THE FOLLY OF THE CROSS

THE FOLLY OF THE CROSS

BY RAOUL PLUS, S.J.

Translated by

IRENE HERNAMAN

THE NEWMAN PRESS
WESTMINSTER, MARYLAND
1949

NIHIL OBSTAT:

Fr. Innocentius Apap, O.P., S.T.M.,
Censor deputatus.

IMPRIMATUR:

Edm. Can. Surmont,
Vicarius generalis.

Westmonasterii,
Die 21a Junii, 1927.

CONTENTS

INTRODUCTION

THE theme of this work is " The Folly of the Cross "; and by the Cross I mean not the Cross of Christ himself, but the cross of his disciples. The folly of which I speak consists in a generous, whole-hearted, effective love for suffering of every kind, whether mental or physical, which certain chosen souls conceive with a view to a closer union with their divine Master, and a more intimate co-operation with him in the great work of the Redemption. This love does not always reveal itself in acts of heroism—that were impossible—but it is always prepared and longing for them. The model of these ardent lovers is our Lord crowned with thorns, with wounded hands and feet, his side pierced with the lance.

Human nature, apart from grace, has little to attract our admiration. Man unaided is very weak and pleasure-loving. What ennobles our race is the fact that in our midst there are some disciples of Christ who love the Cross, and love it with extraordinary fervour. These, indeed, do much for the glory of God. " Grace," says Pascal, " is necessary to make a man a saint. To doubt this is to know nothing of sanctity, and nothing of human nature." What shall we say, then, of these saints—whether publicly honoured by the Church or not—whose ambition it is to reproduce in their own lives as closely as possible the sufferings of Christ ?

Such souls have existed in every age of the Christian era. Need we mention St Paul ? The very title of this work is an echo of that Apostle's

impetuous cry.[1] St Andrew, too, is among the
ardent lovers of the Cross. At the sight of the
Cross erected for his martyrdom, "Hail," he cries
joyfully, "Cross consecrated by the body of Christ,
Cross, upon which his members, glorious and bright as
pearls, were borne, . . . I come to thee; receive me.
Joyous and triumphant, I come to thee. O blessed
Cross, that I have so dearly loved, so constantly
desired." Remember St Ignatius, the Bishop of
Antioch, who, just before he was led away to be
delivered to the wild beasts, wrote to the Romans:
"The world to me is naught. To die in Jesus Christ
is what I deserve above all. Let me copy in myself
the sufferings of my God. Those who have him in
their hearts will understand my desire. My love is
crucified. Nothing now binds me to the earth."

Our Lord asked Blessed Jacopone da Todi, the
reputed author of the *Stabat Mater*, why he had made
himself such a fool in the eyes of men. He replied:
"Because thou wast a greater fool than I."

During the last century, in the year 1825, there
was born in the neighbourhood of Cannes a sailor
called Clement Roux.[2] The world hardly knew his
name, yet he was one of these sublime fools whom
Christ alone can produce. After several years of an
aimless existence, he became enamoured of the Cross.
"Whichever way you choose to take me," he said to
his astonished friends, "I am a fool; so I prefer to
be a fool for the love of God than to please the
world." For twenty-five years, like St Lydwine
before him, he made reparation for his own sins and
for the sins of others, by a life of intense suffering.

---

[1] 1 Cor. i 23. The literal meaning of the text is that
"the Cross appears to the Gentiles an act of folly." It is
only by adaptation, sanctioned by long use, that it comes
to mean that Christ's love for us, manifested by his death
on the Cross, amounts almost to folly.

[2] *Le Saint homme de Grasse, Clement Roux*, by P.
Lambert.

" My God, I love thee passionately and to the point of folly," cried the Foundress of the *Gardiennes Adoratrices du Saint Sacrement*. " I can rightly use these words since worldlings address them to those whom they love, only they are foolish to fix their affections upon feeble imperfect creatures, while I am wise in loving thee."[1]

Father Lourdel, before he joined the White Fathers, in his youth paid a visit to the basilica of St Denys, the ancient burial-place of the kings of France. When he came upon the tomb of Louis X, called the Headstrong, he looked at it for a moment, then he said: " No one thought of blaming you because your passion for playing ball was the cause of your death. Yet we are treated as madmen because we desire to sacrifice our lives for the conversion of the heathen. How senseless the world is !"[2]

To come down to our own times, there was a cavalry officer in the Great War who was wounded in one of the early encounters and later sent to Salonica. The love of the Cross produced such an impression upon his mind that he wrote to a friend saying: " The folly of the Cross means that you feel as if your heart were all on fire. It is as if you saw great waves launched upon you by the Holy Spirit, waves that drive you down into the depths to raise you again to the heights of heaven. You hear divine harmonies that delight your soul and cause it to vibrate beneath the divine touch. You have a faint glimpse of the blood-red glories of sacrifice. Your eyes become so dazzled by the vision of Calvary that you cannot withdraw yourself from the Cross; you become one with it, you are absorbed in it. You look to where the two arms of the Cross meet; it is the meeting of the love of Jesus and of suffering mankind. In a final embrace you drink deep of his

[1] *Journal*, 1851.   [2] *Vie*, by the Abbé Nicq, p. 17.

suffering, it becomes part of yourself.   You want to
be a suffering being, a man of sorrows, after the
likeness of the Man of Sorrows."

On another occasion he wrote: " It is by prayer
and love of the Cross that we shall merit the honour
of uniting our life with that of Christ.   What men
call wisdom, knowledge, intelligence, is nothing but
a world of darkness where they can see but to satisfy
sensual desire; and for them the folly of the Cross is
folly indeed.   They do not understand it.   But it
becomes a shining beacon to them when once their
eyes are opened, when, with quickened heart-beats,
they hear the voice that calls them to eternal bliss.
All through life the folly of the Cross must become
an ever intenser reality both in ourselves and in our
relation to others.   Lord, so love thy servant that his
Cross may one day reach the degree of folly in which
his spirit of detachment and his interior life become
so real that thou wilt vouchsafe to receive him into
thy divine embrace."[1]

These are the facts—or some of them—for we
could multiply examples.   What is the explana-
tion ?   " Granted that the body may be governed
by force, what of the spirit ?   The symbol that has
exercised the greatest influence on the spirit of man
is the symbol of an instrument of torture, the cross.
What power, then, is mighty enough to draw the
eyes of all men to the cross, to enkindle in all the
desire of self-sacrifice ?   The tide witnesses to the
attraction of an orb beyond the clouds.   Shall the
unceasing tide of souls alone rise to an empty
heaven ?"[2]

No, heaven is not empty.   Look at the horizon;
the red ball of the setting sun throws up in relief
the familiar outline of the cross, whereon the Word

---

[1] *Les Étapes de Dehival dans les voies de l'amour*, by
Henri Bontoux, pp. 105, 359.

[2] De Curel, *La nouvelle Idole*.

INTRODUCTION

made flesh has just yielded up his life. It was some days ago that the Roman pro-consul gave the order for three sycamore trees to be cut down, three sycamores for three condemned men. And one of the condemned was the Saviour of the World. "Without shedding of blood there is no remission."[1] Every generous mind can understand the meaning of these words, and the example of Calvary. Throughout the centuries every act of generosity owes its inspiration to him who from his pierced side sheds forth a wondrous light, so piercing in its intensity and yet so benign. It is in him that the divine history of the world centres, in him whom we call the King and centre of all hearts. It has ever been and ever will be the desire of devout souls to have so intense a love of the Passion that it becomes gradually a part of their lives. It must not be supposed that they have an unhealthy desire for suffering as an end in itself: they regard it as a means—and the best means available—of finding love, of inviting Love, and of union with Love itself.

The well-known text of St Paul: "For I judged not myself to know anything among you, but Jesus Christ, and him crucified,"[2] is interpreted by some persons as implying that suffering as an end in itself is an integral part of the gospel teaching. St Paul preached Christ crucified; but only that later he might present to us Christ triumphant. We must be united to his Cross to be sharers in his triumph. In other words, St Paul's gospel is always the good tidings, "the light of the gospel of the glory of Christ," who is the image of God.[3]

When we look at the Crucifixion, we should never fail to see our Lord as he was on Easter morning. But unfortunately we are only too ready to forget

[1] Heb. ix 22; Eph. i 7; Col. i 14.
[2] 1 Cor. ii 2.
[3] 2 Cor. iv 4.

that before Christ entered into glory he underwent
his Passion, and that we also must mount the hill of
Calvary.   Therefore St Paul—as, indeed, all those
who understand aright the nature of man—thinks
it necessary to remind us frequently of the obligation of self-sacrifice.   There are certain people in
these days who are on the wrong path; they are very
willing to indulge their fancy for fantastic penances
while neglecting their daily duties.   Others, led
astray by ill-digested ascetical reading that excites
their imaginations, become exalted by fancying that
they are called to be victims, an idea which is often
purely imaginary, and sometimes disastrous in its
consequences.   Some say that such people are only
too common.

The finest things are the most easily counterfeited.
The folly of the Cross must be grafted on a perfectly
sound stock.   If there should be any pre-existing
mental twist, a lack of balance, ill-formed or in-
sufficiently grounded knowledge of asceticism, then
not only is a solid and fruitful interior life an impossibility, but there is grave spiritual danger.
Illusions that are masked under good appearances
are the most dangerous of all.   We must be first
absolutely sane before we become fools for Christ's
sake.

But must this practice be condemned because of
possible abuse ? Must the best and noblest models
be kept in the background because there are some
grotesque caricatures ?

It will be seen that the folly of the Cross, although
unchanging throughout the centuries in the enthusi-
asm which gives it birth, yet varies in accordance
with the spirit of the times.

We may, without being accused of over-ex-
clusiveness, select three periods, in each of which
devotion to our crucified Saviour stands out in bold
relief and takes on a more individual character.

These periods can be roughly divided in this manner:

(i.) The time of St Bernard and of St Francis of Assisi.

(ii.) The time of St Margaret Mary.

(iii.) The present day.

Moreover, the history of this special devotion to the Passion is, we venture to suggest, characterised respectively in each of these periods by special insistence on these aspects: compassion, compensation, completion.

Naturally the history of man cannot be divided into water-tight compartments; it is by imperceptible changes and not by violent upheavals that compensation takes the place of compassion, and completion follows compensation. The transition is gradual, and is never so complete that the characteristics of the previous epoch cannot be traced, often very plainly, in subsequent developments. In each period all three characteristics are present, but not in equal proportions; one always predominates. Unite the three aspects into one, and you have a complete synthesis which you may call, if you will, the philosophy of the love of Christ crucified.

It cannot be expected that these pages will contain a complete and intricate analysis of all that has been written upon the Passion whether by the fathers, the saints, and other ascetical authors, or in the history of the Church.

We have here only a few small pebbles collected along the path which our Lord follows in his secret visit to interior souls. The interest of the theme lies in the fact that the mosaic is not composed of inanimate particles, but of the burning love-offerings of the saints, by means of which our hearts will be enflamed. Our work may be called a bird's-eye view of the subject. Anyone is at liberty to come to earth for a closer inspection, and his research will be richly rewarded. More detailed studies of individual models would do much to confirm our general conclusions. There is little danger, we think, of their being contested.

THE FOLLY OF THE CROSS

PART I

COMPASSION

CHAPTER I

BEFORE THE TIME OF ST BERNARD—CISTERCIAN LOVE OF THE CROSS

I

THE distinguishing mark of the Middle Ages and its chief claim to honour from the point of view of religion is admittedly a deeper appreciation and love of Christ's suffering humanity, an intense devotion to the sacred Passion.

On the evening of Good Friday Christ was taken down from the cross, and our Lady, having received his sacred body and placed it in the tomb, returned with John and Magdalen to Jerusalem. The painter Tissot depicts Mary making her daily pilgrimage to Calvary, revisiting the very spot where the cross had stood, and meditating on her divine Son and us.

To meditate on the Passion was clearly an habitual practice also with the disciples who had been witnesses of our Lord's death upon the Cross. But it was a time for active warfare,[1] rather than for contemplation. First, there is resistance unto blood. Then would come the more subtle dogmatic contest. Few denied the reality of Christ's human nature,[2]

[1] Minucius Felix, *Octavius*, p. 12.
[2] The Docetists, who held that Christ's human nature was not real but apparent, exercised only a passing influence.

it was rather his divinity that was questioned.
The Gnostic heresy had to be denounced, and the
dogmatic difficulties that were perplexing men's
minds explained. It had to be shown against the
Patripassians[1] that God the Son alone suffered; other
Trinitarian heresies had to be refuted; the Church
had to maintain against the Nestorians that our
Lady is the Mother of God; against the Monophysites
that the two natures in Christ are distinct, although
united in the one person. There were the great
controversies concerning grace, entailing the necessity
for study, argument, and the refutation of error.
It was a period of conflict in which there was little
time for contemplation. Christian piety—judging,
at least, from the writings of those times and ab-
stracting from the hidden interior life of pious souls,
which is known only to God—was of a philosophical
and theological character, more of mental polemics
than of vision. Heresy was rampant. It was not
a time for kneeling long before the Cross, but rather
for standing in the arena, back to the Cross, to face
the invading foe. But there were contemplatives
even in those days: St Augustine, in the midst of
his combats with heresy, declares that " one tear
shed for the memory of Christ's Passion is worth
more than a pilgrimage to Jerusalem and a year's
fast upon bread and water." It was rather that the
prayers of these men were in harmony with the
bellicose spirit of the age, or that they would not
condescend to reveal the secrets of their prayer.

We are now at the beginning of the Middle Ages.
The great controversies are over. There is an
occasional skirmish for some outpost, but the front
is fixed and definitely consolidated, and the enemy

[1] *Translator's Note.*—" The Patripassians were heretics
of the first century, who taught that there is but one person
in the Godhead, the Father who was made man."   See
Catholic Dictionary, Scannell, p. 739.

hemmed in. The soldier who has fought bravely has leisure, in time of peace, to meditate upon the cause for which he has striven. And now that he examines it closely, although he has long been familiar with it, it appears to him in a strangely new light.

It must not be forgotten that up to the close of the fourth century the cross was represented without the figure of Christ. There are in existence two reproductions of the crucifixion belonging to the fifth century. In the sixth century the crucifix is seen more frequently, but the sculptured or moulded figure does not represent a naked, dead Saviour. Our Lord is clad in his garments; he is alive, not a bleeding Saviour, but a triumphant Lord.

It was only in the twelfth century that it became customary to represent him as a victim of expiation for the sins of the world. Up to that time even those people who had an attraction for meditation upon the Passion, dared not permit their imagination to be too realistic. Out of respect for our Lord they refused to gaze upon the naked figure, despoiled of its robes, and torn and covered with wounds.

When, about the sixth century, the first crucifix representing Christ in his sufferings was introduced into France, the faithful protested. It was not right, they felt, to represent our Lord in this way; it was a profanation of the sacred Passion.

As time passed, however, men's feelings changed, and piety underwent a gradual transformation. Not only was the representation of the scene of Calvary no longer revolting to the popular eye, but on the contrary it became attractive, and the lyric prose of the writers of that day vibrates with a poignant agony, as may be seen in the following extract from St Bernard:

" Hail, Salvation of the world ! Hail, my beloved Jesu ! Nail me to thy cross, I am longing for it;

thou knowest the cause. Come to my aid. Engrave
thy red wounds, those deep fissures upon my heart,
so that loving thee above all things, I may be pierced
through and through. Look at me, my Beloved,
who art hanging on the cross, draw me to thee and
say: ' I forgive thee all, thou art made whole.' Thy
love has taken possession of me, I embrace thee,
nor heed the blood-stains; I cling to thee; support
me and reproach me not though I deserve it.
Grant that my boldness may not be displeasing to
thee, sick and sin-stained though I be, and may the
precious blood here outpoured wash me and be my
cure and make me without stain."[1]

Another chant gives a wonderful description of the
devout soul stricken with sorrow:

" Innocent Lamb, bathed in the blood whereby
the world was redeemed from sin, hanging upon this
stalwart tree, with arms outstretched to embrace me,
in thy humility thou hast permitted the beauty and
freshness of thy countenance to be dimmed by the
approach of death. Before thy soul takes flight
turn thine eyes towards me, and save me. Look
once again at me. I have arrived at a propitious
moment, when thou art about to distribute thy
goods. . . . And as thou art parting with all thou
hast and disposing of it to everyone I claim my share.
Thou bequeathest to thy mother a son, to the
disciple a mother, to the Father thy spirit, to the
thief eternal life. Shall I be so unfortunate as to be
left unprovided when there are so many legacies ?
I call upon all present to bear witness that thou
dost bow thy head as a sign that my request is granted.
My song must be hushed, my tears will supply all
that remains unsaid. . . . It is not the moment for
singing when the earth and sky are in mourning."[2]

[1] Attributed to St Bernard, and printed at the end of his
works in Mabillon's edition (Paris, 1690, vol. ii, p. 899).
[2] *Mystiques espagnoles*, by Fra Luis de Leon, pp. 302-303.

Even when the scene described is not explicitly sorrowful, as in the Joyful Mysteries, the memory of our Lord's sufferings is always present.

Listen, for example, to the tender expressions used by the disciple of St Bernard, Æbredius, speaking of the loss of the child Jesus in the Temple.

" Where wert thou, little Jesus, during those sad three days ? Who prepared thy food, who made thy bed and tidied thy clothes ? . . . Take great care of thy recovered Treasure, Mary, and give him many kisses to make up for those he was deprived of during his absence."

It is known that our Lord on the Cross was in full enjoyment of the Beatific Vision, so from that point of view he claims our admiration rather than our tears. Thus in the book *De Laudibus Sanctae Crucis*, written by Rhaban Maur, Archbishop of Mainz in the ninth century, our Lord is described as the majestic King. The cross is not an instrument of suffering, rather is it a throne. " Christ, the incarnate God, born among men, was resplendently fair ; he was all beautiful within and without."[1]

This aspect of the Passion is exemplified by the figure of our Lord called " the beautiful Christ," which stands over one of the doorways of Amiens Cathedral ; it does not represent our Lord as he was in the agony in the garden, or in the scourging at the pillar, or in the torment of Golgotha.

On the other hand, if the pious soul is contemplating the true figure of the Crucifixion, it becomes so enraptured that its very sorrow is an ecstasy. To quote the words of Bl. Angela of Foligno:

" One day," she writes, " I was looking at the Cross and the figure on the Cross ; I saw it with my bodily eyes. Suddenly my soul became so inflamed with burning love, that my whole being was filled with joy and happiness. I saw and felt our Lord

[1] Cologne edition, 1626, t. i, p. 313.

embracing me with his crucified arms, and the bliss of it astonished me; it was greater than anything I had ever experienced before. Since that moment there has remained . . . a wonderful sense of joy in my soul which continues; this dazzling experience outshines any I have ever known. When I am enfolded in this embrace, the joy that is communicated to my soul is such that it would be useless to attempt to sorrow with our Lord in his sufferings, although I see before me the pierced hands of Christ crucified. Sometimes he presses me so closely to him that my soul seems to enter into his wounded side, and the joy is such that no human words can express it. It was so overpowering that my legs became unable to support me, and I was thrown to the ground. . . . This happened to me on one occasion in the square of St Mary's. A scene from the Passion was being acted, and it might have been imagined I should weep, but on the contrary I was filled with a superhuman joy, which so increased that I lost the power of speech and fell to the ground as if thunderstruck. I was vouchsafed a dazzling vision. . . . It seemed to me that my soul entered into the wound of our Lord's side, and in this wound, instead of feeling sorrow, I was inebriated with a joy that baffles description."[1]

All early writers, however, do not show the same serene happiness in their aspirations; very few enjoyed the consolations of Bl. Angela of Foligno In many cases the love of Christ crucified has a more tragic note. What they see is that Christ suffered on Calvary; what they desire is to suffer with him.

"What hast thou done, my sweetest Jesus, to be treated thus ? It is I who caused thy death. I am the instrument of thy Passion and its torments. . . . O my unhappy soul, gaze, gaze upon thy horrible

[1] *Book of the Visions and Instructions*, French translation by Hello, xxxvi, p. 173.

crime, and stir up within thee fear and sorrow."[1]
Thus prayed St Anselm, and his devotion to our Lord's
sufferings was the inspiration of many anonymous
writings of the Passion traditionally attributed to
him.   Yet in spite of these aspirations, St Anselm's
writings on the Passion have not the force of those
of St Bernard.

II

St Bernard and St Francis are the two great
exponents of the folly of the Cross in the Middle
Ages.   Their influence was enormous, for both were
fathers of a large posterity, among which are
numbered many saints.   Up to their time specula-
tion predominated.   With them it is love that holds
the first place.   Without doubt their success was
due, in the first instance, to their holiness, and in
the second place to their special spiritual endowments.   But it was attributable also to their
ecstatic devotion to our Lord in his Passion.

Tradition says of St Bernard that the Passion of
our Lord was his delight.   He would often pray
before a crucifix, and sometimes when the Saint was
in a transport our Lord was seen to loosen his hands
from the cross to support him.

Innumerable were the tender ejaculations which
the scenes of the Passion evoked from the Founder
of the Cistercian Order.

Among the mysteries of the holy Infancy, it was
for the Circumcision that St Bernard showed preference.   It was the first time that our Lord shed his
blood.   The name of Jesus signifies Saviour.   And
the name of Mary's divine Son inspired many
outpourings of burning love from the Saint.

He confided to his monks that having no personal
good merits to offer to God, he used to make a

[1] St Anselm, Meditations, III and IV *De Humanitate
Christi* (Migne, P.L. clviii, 725-758).

spiritual bouquet of all the bitterness and anguish
suffered by our Lord during his earthly life: his
privations as a child, the labours of his ministry,
the weariness of his journeyings, his nights of prayer,
the temptation after his fast in the wilderness, his
sufferings at his betrayal, the denial, the insults and
the blows, the mockery and the nails.

It may be surmised that St Bernard had a greater
devotion for the agony on Calvary than for the
poverty of Bethlehem. He says of himself: " To
know Jesus, and him crucified, is the summit of my
philosophy."[1]

The disciples of St Bernard still preserve the tender
devotion of their founder for Christ crucified.

In the composition entitled *The Mystic Vine*,[2] the
writer mourns over the innocent Jesus called to suffer
from the beginning of his life upon earth.

" Eight days after his birth and already his blood
is flowing! What a piteous sight !" Then he pro-
ceeds to describe the scourging and crucifixion.

" They put on him a purple robe, but he has what
is better still, the vesture of his blood-stained flesh,
the purple garment of his own blood. Two baths
suffice to dye a robe, but the body of Christ must
needs be immersed a third time. After the agony
and the scourging, there was the crucifixion. See,
O Christian soul, thy Spouse all ruddy; look closely,
is this his tunic, canst thou recognise it ? Alas !
a wild beast has torn his flesh; and he is thy son,
thy brother and thy spouse."

The moral lesson which follows the contemplation is that since Christ, the Head, has suffered so
much, the members of Christ must suffer with him.
The title of the work, *The Mystic Vine*, indicates
the same truth. It deals with the great doctrine

[1] *In Cantica*, serm. xliii, 4.
[2] Works of St Bernard, Venetian edition, 1727; t. iii.
Vitis Mystica, seu Tractatus de Passione Domini.

of our incorporation with Christ. Therefore the monk continues:

" The body of Christ is crushed, let us learn how to subdue our bodies; the soul will become more beautiful after the resemblance of our Lord's beauty. Our bodies must be confirmed to the likeness of our Lord's wounded body, so that our souls may resemble the shining splendour of Jesus. Let us say with St Paul: ' I am crucified with Christ. I bear the marks of the Lord Jesus in my body.' "[1]

And what is true of bodily penance is still truer of interior mortification.

" We are troubled by the obstacles we encounter. Let us look at our Chief when he was insulted, and cease complaining. We ought to bear patiently all that irritates us, so as to be worthy members of the Head."

Another monk of the same Order, Abbot Geoffrey, in his Commentary on the works of St Bernard, writes much in the same strain:

" Dare we seek for pleasure and honours when Christ suffered the death and shame of the Cross ? Scourged, spat upon, crowned with thorns, nailed to the hard wood of the Cross between two malefactors, pierced with the lance even after his death ! Is it not a disgrace that, when he suffered all this, a Christian should enjoy a comfortable luxurious life ?"

There are numerous books on the Passion among the apocryphal writings of St Bernard: *The Sufferings of Mary on Calvary ; Meditations on the Passion and Resurrection of our Lord ; Lamentations on the Passion of Christ ; Priestly Instructions on the Passion, the Holy Eucharist and Heaven.* They are not the actual compositions of St Bernard, but they reflect his mind and inspiration.

A century later there is St Gertrude of the Cis-

[1] Gal. vi 17.

tercian[1] monastery of Helfta. Her writings show a close affinity to those of St Bernard. Her rhapsodies on the Sorrowful Mysteries are very touching, and especially those in the fourth book of her *Revelations*.

"On Passion Sunday she made an offering of herself, body and soul, to bear all that it pleased the divine will to send her in honour of his Passion; and it seemed to her that our Lord of his goodness accepted this offering with inexpressible joy. She began then under the impulse of divine grace, to salute each of the sacred members that underwent such torments for our salvation in the Passion. And every time that she saluted one of these members a bright light came from it and illumined all her soul, and in this radiant glory there was imparted to her the gift of innocence which our Lord purchased for his Church through the pains suffered in that member. When she was all illumined with this wondrous light she said: 'O my Lord, teach me by means of this gift of innocence which thou of thy goodness hast freely bestowed upon me how I can worthily celebrate thy sacred Passion.' Our Lord replied: 'Recall to mind frequently with gratitude and compassion the anguish which I thy Creator and Master suffered when I prayed so earnestly that the vehemence of my love caused the ground to be soaked with a sweat of blood. Then in union with the act of submission of my own will when I cried, 'Father, not my will but thine be done,' give over to me all thy works, and everything that concerns thee. Accept all that comes, whether it be prosperity or adversity, as a message of love from me.' "

As the Saint advanced in the realisation of the Sorrowful Mysteries, the greater was her compassion, whereby she became a partaker in the sufferings and merits of her crucified Lord.

[1] According to some this was a Benedictine monastery.

" On the feast of the Last Supper, she passed the whole day in complete recollection so as to be always with our Lord; he presented himself to her as he was on earth on the eve of his Passion. All that day she saw him suffering the agony of death; for being the eternal Wisdom of his Father, he knew beforehand all the sufferings that would befall him; throughout his Passion his sensitive nature tasted the bitterness of death; the pallor of his features and the trembling of his limbs showed the anguish that he was undergoing. This spectacle moved her soul to such grief, to such compassion, that if she had possessed a thousand hearts she would have expended all their energy in sympathising with him, who loved her so greatly. She realised that the violent beating of her heart, caused by the ardour of her love, and the anguish of death, was beating also with redoubled vigour upon the Sacred Heart, and such was the force of these palpitations that she was on the point of sinking. Then our Lord said to her: ' The agony and pain which I endured in my body during my mortal life for love of men, I an suffering today in thy heart, which has been moved to such a depth of compassion by the memory of my sufferings. In return I give thee all the fruits of my Passion and my precious death, for the increase of thy eternal reward. Further, everywhere, wherever it may be, that the wood of the Cross on which I suffered is adored, thou wilt receive the reward of the compassionate love thou hast shown today, and thy heart as well as thy soul will share in it.' "

She tells us that as soon as she heard the clapper sounding the hour for office, her heart beat as if it would burst.

" It was as if she had been told of the approaching decease of some loving and intimate friend and was hastening to assist at his deathbed, so eager was she to retire within herself to meditate upon the Passion of our Lord, and to offer tender sympathy with the sufferings of her Beloved. In this way, by her faithful love, she was enabled to pay back her debt to him for all that he had suffered for her.

Throughout Good Friday and even Holy Saturday, her soul clung so closely to her Beloved, that it was impossible for her to attend to exterior matters. On Good Friday, she tells us that during Terce she became so inflamed with love at the thought that at that very hour our Lord was mocked and crowned with thorns and laden with his cross, that she cried: ' Behold me, my well-Beloved, I offer thee my heart in return for thy love, and to make up even in a small degree for the undeserved sufferings of thy Passion; grant that from this day forward, up to the very hour of my death, I may share in all the sufferings of thy most sweet Heart and thy immaculate body; and if owing to human frailty my memory should for one instant forget thy sufferings, let me feel a sharp pain in my heart to correspond with the bitter pain of thy Passion.' Our Lord replied: ' This desire inspired by thy love for me gives me infinite pleasure. But if thou desirest me to find my full delight in thy heart, leave me free to give thee what I wish, and do not ask for either joy or sorrow.' "

This sentence contains a valuable piece of advice. There are certain generous-minded souls who wonder whether it is allowable to ask for suffering. St Gertrude, or rather our Lord through her lips, settles the question. There are cases where the attraction for suffering makes it permissible to ask for it; but they always require careful investigation. A generous soul, whatever may befall it, can always resolve to abandon itself into God's hands. In this way the danger of vanity or imprudent action is minimised, and the soul more closely resembles our

Lord himself, who said: " My meat is to do the will of him that sent me."[1]

A recent historian of St Gertrude, Father Dolan of Downside Abbey, tells us that one night she was almost intoxicated with love for our Lord, but making an effort to control herself, she put down the crucifix she was holding, and wished our Lord good-night, saying: " Permit me, Lord, to sleep so as to recuperate my body, for it has lost all its vigour during this heavenly converse." Our Lord then detached his right arm from the cross, and put it round St Gertrude's neck.

The Saint had not waited to receive this great favour before offering to our Lord her acts of adoration and compassion.

"Infinitely merciful Saviour, mark with thy precious blood the imprint of thy wounds upon my heart, so that I may learn both thy love and thy sorrow, and that the memory of thy wounds may be permanently engraven there, awaken in me grief for thy Passion, and enkindle in me the fire of thy love."[2]

The next passage brings us in touch with the devotion to the Sacred Heart.

" Most loving Saviour, by the merit of thy pierced Heart, pierce also the heart of Gertrude with the darts of thy love, so that nothing earthly may remain there, that it may be filled with thy divine love."[2]

St Bridget of Sweden, although not belonging to the Cistercian Order, was a Cistercian in mind, because of her great devotion to the cross.

As spouse and mother she decided with the consent of her husband to observe continency, so that they might both enter the religious life. Ulf, the husband, died a Cistercian in the monastery of Alvastra in the year 1344, and thenceforward

---

[1] St John iv 34.
[2] *The Herald of Divine Love*, Book II, ch. iv.

St Bridget gave herself up more and more to our Lord in his Passion.

At the age of ten she had had a vision of Christ on the cross. It was after hearing a sermon on the Passion; he said to her: "See how they have treated me." And she answered: "Lord, who have treated thee thus?" "Those who despise and disdain my love." From that day St Bridget could never think about the Passion without weeping, and her descriptions of the sufferings of our Lord are as realistic as anything that can be found in the writings of the Middle Ages.

To her songs of exaltation over the Passion she joined the prose of a crucified life. As a young married woman she had a sumptuous bed in her room. Suddenly one night she heard a voice saying: "On the cross I had no place whereon to rest. Thou, on the contrary, seekest for ease and repose." From that moment, whenever her husband was absent, she slept upon the floor for the whole night.[1]

CHAPTER II

ST FRANCIS OF ASSISI AND HIS DISCIPLES—THE DOMINICAN INFLUENCE

I

SIDE by side with St Bernard in his love of the Cross stands St Francis of Assisi. For him also our Lord performed the same miracle as he did for St Gertrude, when he detached his arm from the Cross and lovingly embraced the Poor Man of Assisi, who henceforth, like his Master, bore in his flesh the imprint of the nails.

[1] *Vie*, by Countess de Flavigny, p. 38.

"I am the herald of the great King!" cried St Francis. The great King is he who was crowned with thorns: for the disciple nothing will be too hard or austere, for the likeness between Master and disciple must be real and deep. The first account of the Friars Minor describes him as living with his companions in absolute poverty and reduced to eating the turnips given in charity to the friars by the inhabitants of Assisi to save them from dying of hunger.[1]

It is well known how this "fool of the Cross" treated his brother Ass, as he called his body.

The commencement of the folly of the Cross for the Poor Man of Assisi dates from the miracle of the crucifix of San Damiano. It was in the year 1226, during the fair, and Francis, who was then twenty-four years of age, had just returned from Foligno and had entered the Church of San Damiano. He was lying prostrate before the crucifix when suddenly he became inflamed with love for our Lord. He saw the Christ on the crucifix moving his lips, and a voice said: "Francis, go and repair my house which is falling into ruins." From that hour, Thomas of Celano tells us, "compassion for our crucified Lord was imprinted on his soul." The "legend of St Bonaventura" declares that when St Francis was despoiled of his coat before the Bishop of Assisi, he was given an old gardener's cloak. Before putting it on, he cut it into the shape of a cross.

Later, it was not only upon his body but in his body that he bore the marks of Christ crucified. But before the imprint of the stigmata appeared upon his hands, it was engraven in his heart.

He composed an office of the Passion from verses from the Bible.

"O all ye that pass by the way, attend and see if there be any sorrow like to my sorrow."[2]

[1] Thomas of Celano, *Legenda prima*, ch. xvi.
[2] Lam. i 12.

"For many dogs have encompassed me: the council of the malignant hath besieged me."[1]

"They parted my garments among them: and upon my vesture they cast lots. They have dug my hands and feet. They have numbered all my bones."[2]

"They gave me gall for my food; and in my thirst they gave me vinegar to drink."[3]

"Thou hast brought me to the dust of death. I am poured out like water, all my bones are scattered."[4]

After the vision of San Damiano, wherein our Lord revealed to St Francis the terrible plight of those souls who are perishing, in spite of the sacrifice on Calvary, he could never think of the Passion without weeping.

Sometimes his sobs became overpowering, and on one occasion a man who overheard his lamentations asked him what was the matter. "Alas!" cried St Francis, "I am weeping over the Passion of my Lord Jesus Christ." And as his questioner remained dumbfounded, he continued: "I ought not to be ashamed to go through the world weeping in this manner."[5]

The words of St Paul: "It pleased God, by the foolishness of our preaching, to save them that believe,"[6] were verified in their fulness by St Francis.

His vehement preaching of Christ crucified attracted the attention of a young girl belonging to the important family of the Sciffi of Assisi. She came in search of the Saint, and asked permission to be enrolled under the banner of poverty. St

[1] Ps. xxi 17.   [2] Ibid., 19, 18.
[3] Ibid., lxviii 22.   [4] Ibid., xxi 15, 16.
[5] St Francis is the author of the familiar invocation of the Stations of the Cross: "We adore thee, O Christ, and we bless thee, because by thy holy Cross thou hast redeemed the world."
[6] 1 Cor. i 21.

Francis answered: " If thou desirest me to believe in thee, put on a sack and go through the town begging for bread." Clare—for it was she—obeyed. The people of Assisi did not recognise her in this unwonted garb, but St Francis knew who it was. This was the beginning of the order of the Poor Clares.

St Clare (1194-1252), during the whole of her life, had a remarkable devotion to the Five Wounds. For a long period it was her custom to meditate upon the Passion every day from midday until three o'clock. One Maundy Thursday, while she was contemplating the sufferings of our Lord, she fell into an ecstasy and did not come to herself until Saturday evening. Her favourite prayer was: " Praise and glory be rendered to thee, O most loving Jesus, for the sacred wound in thy right hand. Praise and glory . . . for the sacred wound of thy left hand. Praise and glory . . . for the sacred wound in thy adorable feet, in thy side," etc.

The preaching of the Franciscan Friars was to arouse in the Christian world a burning love for Christ crucified. Before this time there had indeed been some isolated writings in honour of the Passion. Now the love of the Cross would grow and flourish wherever the sons of the Poor Man came. The contemplation of the sacred wounds was to become the favourite devotion of Christian souls.

His followers speak frequently of the Passion. Jacopone da Todi gives an imaginary dialogue between our Lord on the cross and the devout soul.

"Look at me for a moment . . . on the cross where I suffered so greatly to prove to thee the ardour of my divine love. . . . Thou art written in my heart in letters of blood. . . . It was my love for thee that constrained me to come into the world; my Sacred Heart did not shrink even from the pains of death. . . . Thou seest my hands and my feet, my bleeding head, my whole body tortured with pain; but even more grievous to me is it that thou canst witness the sufferings of me thy Redeemer, and think them of no account." And the soul answers: " To whom should I give myself but to thee my Spouse ?   In thee alone may I hope; may thy love consume me.   Thy life and death show plainly the measureless depth of the love which consumes thy heart."[1]

The author of the *Stimulus Amoris*[2] treats almost exclusively of the Passion; he shows how vain it is to seek for contemplation and to leave out the cross.

" I desire never to be separated from Jesus on the cross.   It is good to remain with him, and in him I wish to build three tabernacles, one in his hands, another in his feet, and the third in his side, and to stay there for ever.   There I will speak to his heart, and obtain all my desires.   O wounds so tenderly loved !   How blind are the children of Adam, who know not how to draw close to our Lord by way of his wounds !"

The writings of St Bonaventura (1221-1274) closely resemble those of his father, St Francis.   The following passages are applicable to everyone who has a right understanding of the Gospels.

" When the Christian contemplates our Lord hanging on the Cross in agony for love of us, all else seems easy to bear, provided he is able to live for Jesus Christ and to please him.   When he sees how our Lord has loved him, and the insults and torments that Christ has endured for him, he is inflamed with love for his Redeemer.   His soul is on fire with love, and he longs with all his heart to suffer and die with Jesus Christ.   He desires that the Passion may

---

[1] Bainvel, *Devotion to the Sacred Heart*, p. 145.
[2] Long attributed to St Bonaventura.   The editor of the latter's works (Quaracchi, 1902) attributes it to James of Milan, friar minor.

become a part of his life, and longs to become transformed after the likeness of his crucified Master."

His favourite ejaculatory prayer was: " O my God, may I see thee on the Cross always, whichever way I turn, and may everything around me appear empurpled with thy blood."

His fervent aspirations were due to those hours of secret prayer passed in contemplation of the crucifix.

Another son of St Francis was John de Caulibus, who has been called the pseudo-Bonaventura; he loved to dwell upon every detail of our Lord's suffering life.

He meditates as follows on the tears of the child Jesus.

" Do you think that his mother could restrain her tears when she saw him weeping ? She must have wept also. Her son lying on her breast, and seeing her tears, stretched out his little hands towards her mouth, and passed them over her face, as if begging her to moderate her grief. . . . Mary on her part comforted him with words and caresses. And out of compassion for his mother, he controlled his sobs."

This naïve little sketch is followed by a forcible word-picture of the Passion: " One of the men seizes Jesus, another binds him . . . another pushes him, another curses him, another spits in his face. . . ."[1]

The following chapters give the development of each of these points. One special volume is devoted to a commentary on the Seven Words on the Cross. The pious monk also composed a kind of Litany, entitled *Praises in Honour of the Holy Cross*, and wrote as its dedication the following lines: " Grant, O Jesus crucified, that all through my life I may find my delight in weeping over thy death."

Even when he is exultant as in *The Tree of Life*, a third of his pious labours is devoted to the sorrowful mysteries.

[1] *Mediationes vitæ Christi*, lxxiv, lxxxiv.

The sons and daughters of St Francis were apostles of the Cross not only by their words but also by their example. Mention has been made already of the tertiary Bl. Angela of Foligno, but we cannot speak of the love of the Cross without referring to her again.

As a married woman and a mother, she saw everything that she had taken from her. As she voluntarily submitted to each successive sacrifice, our Lord rewarded her with fresh lights and graces. Rarely has a soul received such revelations concerning the suffering manhood of Christ. Her ecstatic flights and intuitions are those of the Seraphim. At the same time, she was given the unique power of expressing these divine revelations in human language.

Here are a few examples:

" ' If thou desirest to reach the Cross,' said the Holy Spirit to me, ' strip thyself of everything.' I had to forgive every offence and despoil myself of all earthly things . . . even of my very self and my own self-possession. . . . For the first time I renounced my rich clothes, my elaborate hairdressing, and my dainty food." God helped her in her self-annihilation by taking to himself, one by one, her mother, her husband and her sons.

" I was led to practise such hard penances that I cannot describe them. But as I found it incompatible with the life in the world, I resolved to give up everything and follow the divine inspiration which was leading me to the Cross. . . . The desire for poverty came to me . . . but I was tormented by a thousand misgivings . . . I should die of hunger, or I should perish with cold; everyone would disapprove of what I was doing. Then I made up my mind to take this step, whatever harm might befall me."

She tells us that of her meditations upon the

Passion there was born in her " a fresh desire to strip herself of everything." People tried to oppose her designs, but she declared: " Neither all the good nor all the evil in the whole world could hold me back. . . . I felt that I could keep nothing for myself. . . ." The day when she sold her country-house and gave the money to the poor, was the first occasion when she experienced " transports of love." She could no longer bear to look at a scene from the Passion.

God sent every kind of trial, both of body and soul, to purify her, especially interior trials, and in particular a temptation to " wicked humility "—*i.e.*, despair.

She went in search of opportunities of practising mortification. We all know the terrible appearance of a person suffering from leprosy. " After having pressed her face against the leper's face," she declared, " it seemed to me as wonderful as if I had just received Holy Communion; I cannot express the joy that filled my soul." And she adds: " If anyone is nervous at the commencement of a life of penance, I can bear witness to the joys that await him once he has started."

At times our Lord rewarded her with intimate revelations of his Passion.

" He appeared to me . . . on the cross: ' Look at me,' he cried, ' and see my wounds.' And in some wonderful way he showed me how he had suffered everything for me. This occurred several times. He displayed each of his sufferings one after the other in detail, and said to me: ' What canst thou do for me in return ?' He revealed to me the pains in his head, the torment that he suffered when the hairs of his eyebrows and of his beard were torn out. He counted the blows of the scourges, and showed me exactly the spot where each of them struck him, and said: ' It was for thee, for thy sake.' And still he continued, displaying the sufferings of his Passion and repeating the words: 'What canst thou do in return?' And I wept and wept, and sobbed."

With each act of generosity, our Lord gave her fresh revelations. "The Passion lay spread out before my eyes. I begged of our Lord that I might shed my blood for his sake, as he had shed his blood for me. . . . I wished to die for love of him, and because he had died upon the cross, I asked the grace to die in some other more horrible manner. . . . I could not imagine a form of death that was sufficiently shameful to satisfy my desires."

On several occasions, the Saint begged our Lady and St John to obtain for her the privilege of suffering the pains of our Lord, or, at any rate, those which they themselves had been allowed to endure. They obtained this favour for her once, and she confesses that day was one of the most terrible in her whole life.

From that time forward, she had finished with the world: "My heart was enclosed in the Passion of Christ."

Can we be surprised that the first editors of the works of Bl. Angela of Foligno called them *The Theology of the Cross*?[1] Another Franciscan tertiary, St Margaret of Cortona, born in the year 1247, was for a long time a sinner before she became a passionate lover of Christ crucified. The good Master asked of her the thrice-repeated question that he had asked of St Peter:

"Margaret, lovest thou me?" "Ah, Lord, not merely do I love thee, but I desire to dwell in thy heart." "Enter there, and make it thy refuge." Then again he cries: "Margaret, lovest thou me?" She was troubled, and said hesitatingly: "No, Lord." "When wilt thou love me, then?" "When I experience all the pains of the Passion." Again a

[1] Pavia, 1538.

third time came the question: " Margaret, lovest thou me?" And the answer: "No, Lord, for if I loved thee, I should serve thee better. I desire, at least, to be able to shed my blood as a proof of my love." " Dost thou wish, like St Andrew, to die on the cross?" " As it pleases thee, Lord, provided I die of love and am crucified with thee."[1]

On another occasion our Lord said to her: " Keep the door of my temple (thy soul) carefully shut, and fasten the lock with the key of my Passion." On another occasion he congratulated her upon having chosen for her lot the crown of thorns and the scorn of the crucifixion.

At a later date, about the year 1390, Battista Varani, prioress of Camerino in Umbria, wrote a book on the interior sufferings of Christ in his Passion (*Dolori mentali di Cristo*). These meditations deal with the sorrow which our Lord experienced at the thought of the sins of the lost, the sins of the elect, the sorrows of Mary, the sin of Judas, the ingratitude of the Jews and others, and the love of Magdalen and his disciples. The volume had a wide circulation and did much to inspire the Christians of the sixteenth and seventeenth centuries with a devotion to Christ, victim for our sins.

The influence of St Francis of Assisi was not confined to these individuals. Under his inspiration, artists were moved to show their love for our Lord's Passion in their art. Numerous pictures of the Passion appeared, and these, as well as the preaching of the Passion, contributed to producing a greater and more widely spread devotion to our Lord's sufferings among the general public.

Fifty years after the death of St Francis, Cimabue, in the full vigour of his artistic talent, was seeking to depart from the severe rigidity of the Byzantine style. He decorated the tomb of the Saint, and

[1] *Life*, by Leopold de Chérancé, xvii, p. 144.

placed in a prominent position his fresco of the crucifixion, in which he abandoned the stiff heraldic pose so common at that period in favour of a more supple and natural style. Giotto completed and perfected the transition. He had a predilection for painting our Lord on the Cross; and this not so much for the love of art, as for the love of Christ crucified.

The Umbrian school of painting is marked with the imprint of the Passion.

Devotion to our Lord's sufferings flourished under varied forms, as a consequence of the Cistercian and Franciscan influence.

It is at this period that the devotion to the Five Wounds makes its appearance. We have already read the sayings of St Bernard and his disciples, of St Clare, and of St Gertrude. St Bonaventura declares that he approaches " the humble Heart of the most high Lord through the open portal of his pierced side.''

It was rare—as we have already remarked— before the eighth century, to find our Lord represented on the cross. There were no wounds in his side, and in place of the crown of thorns, our Saviour wore a royal crown. A change was brought about by the crusaders who returned from Palestine with the thought of Christ's sufferings imprinted upon their minds, and gradually pictures of the crucifixion and of the Ecce Homo began to multiply. Everyone could not visit the Holy Land, but if the principal scenes of the Passion were represented, people would be assisted in trying to picture the sufferings of our Saviour hour by hour. Hence the devotion of the Stations of the Cross was inaugurated.

Nor was pictorial art the sole method of visualizing the Passion. There were the mystery plays. In 1402 Charles VI made a grant of letters patent to the

confraternity of the Passion. The faithful crowded
to see the mystery plays, and were moved to tears
by them. " It seems," writes E. Mâle, " as if the
whole of Christendom had received the gift of
tears."[1]

Pictures began to appear in which our Lord is
showing his wounded side. From the display of
the wound to making visible his heart is but a step.
Already our Lord was preparing the Christian world
for the great revelations of Paray-le-Monial. Pictures of the pierced heart with the wounded hands
and feet on either side were spread abroad, notably
in Germany, and only finally disappeared when they
were proscribed—with all images—by the Lutherans
at the Reformation.

Moreover, our Lord was secretly initiating one or
two privileged souls in the devotion to the Sacred
Heart; so that when in the year 1689 it was made
known, it was not as some persons imagined entirely
new.

The author of *The Mystic Vine* tells us to " love,
cherish and embrace our wounded Saviour with all
our strength, for his hands and feet and side and
heart have been furrowed as if with the ploughshare
by the hands of the wicked."

His desire was to dwell always in the Sacred Heart:

" Receive my prayer into the sanctuary of thy
mercy, or better still, take my whole self and receive
me into thy heart."

For what other purpose was the Sacred Heart
pierced, if not to be a refuge for those souls who wish
to spend their lives in loving and in suffering with
him ?

The author of the *Imitation* later gives echo to
these strains. St Mary Magdalen de Pazzi, in her
convent at Florence, was often moved with pity at
the thought of " the grief and compassion which

[1] *L'Art religieux de la fin du Moyen Age en France*, p. 82.

filled the Sacred Heart " at the sight of so many men from whom his precious blood would have been shed in vain.

Some of the secret communications made to Bl. Angela of Foligno have been mentioned already. She tells us:

" Christ revealed himself to me, and gave me a deep knowledge of himself. I could not sleep. He called me, and bid me put my lips to his wounded side. I seemed to do so, and to drink of his blood, and in that life-blood I was cleansed."

A century and a half earlier the same favour was granted to St Lutgarde. On several occasions our Lord revealed his Sacred Heart to her, and invited her to kiss the wound.

The cult of the Precious Blood was by no means one of the lesser devotions of that period. Of this St Catherine of Siena, the Dominican tertiary, is the chief exponent.

II

In the minds of St Lutgarde and Bl. Angela of Foligno the memory of the Precious Blood was intermittent. With St Catherine it was a constant thought, an hourly pang; it haunted her.

From a certain date onwards, her letters always began with the words: " I am writing to you in the Precious Blood." She advised her confessor, Raymond of Capua, " to plunge into the blood of Christ crucified, to become inebriated with it, to clothe himself with it, to grow strong in it."[1]

In the second volume of her *Letters*, she writes: " I desire the precious blood to be with me in my work."[2]

To a monk who had deserted his Order, she speaks of the " key of Christ's blood which you have thrown into the abyss."[3]

---

[1] *Letter cxlvi*, p. 442.   [2] *Letter cxxxix*, p. 421.
[3] *Letter clxxx*, p. 65.

And again to her confessor: "Always have the blood of Christ before your eyes, to urge you to the combat. Let your will be reduced to nought and perish in this glorious life-stream, so that being dead, it may no longer fall into temptation."[1]

Speaking of the priestly office, she accommodates the words of our Lord to St Peter, "I will give to thee the keys of the kingdom of heaven,"[2] to mean "the keys of the Precious Blood." Her prayer to the "Eternal Blood," which comes at the end of her *Dialogues*, should be read. She states plainly her faith in the supremacy of the Precious Blood. Her one desire is to shed the blood of her own veins for our Lord. She is ashamed to be living as she does. "I am but a vile slave in this world where the blood of martyrs has flowed for love of the Precious Blood."[3]

A final passage, in which she speaks of the folly of the Cross, deserves special mention.

"O divine Mercy, that proceedest from the eternal Father, it is by thee that we have been created and recreated in the Blood of thy Son; it is thy mercy which caused thy Son to die in agony and to be abandoned on the wood of the cross. In the heights of heaven thy saints reveal thy mercy. If I look to earth, there thy mercy abounds. In hell also thy mercy is shown, because thou dost not inflict upon the damned a torment so great as their crimes. O divine Folly! was it not sufficient for thee to become incarnate that thou must die for us? And thy mercy has done even more than this, for thou hast given thyself to be our food. O divine Mercy! my heart is on fire at the thought of thee. Thy mercy enfolds me whichever way I turn."[4]

Another Catherine, also a Dominican, but a simple tertiary, was St Catherine of Ricci, who died in the

---

[1] *Letter clxviii*, p. 65.
[2] St Matt. xvi 19.
[3] *Letter cxlvii*, p. 451.
[4] *Dialogues*, xxx.

year 1590. She had an insatiable love for her
crucified Master. When she was at school at the
convent of St Peter of Morticelli, she spent long
hours gazing at the crucifix which hung behind the
nuns' grill. Sometimes the figure would come to
life and talk to her. Later on, when she became a
daughter of St Dominic, her love for the Passion
increased in intensity, and God granted her the
grace of the stigmata.

During a period of twelve years, from 1542 to
1554, she fell into an ecstasy every Thursday from
midday until four o'clock on Friday. Body and
soul, she partook in detail of the sufferings of the
Passion. Her biographer tells us " that so complete
was her abandonment to her Beloved that her
loving transports were inexhaustible."[1]

Another Dominican tertiary was St Rose of Lima,
the little South American, who was often consoled
by apparitions of St Catherine of Siena. The
penances which she imposed upon herself out of love
for her crucified Saviour are most extraordinary.
She wore a spiked iron band round her head, she
carried a heavy cross for long hours upon her
shoulders that were already bleeding from the
discipline, she slept upon a bed of potsherds and
sharp-pointed stones. Sometimes she would pass
the whole night with her arms fastened by two
nails to a cross, and remain there suspended while
she united her prayers to those of our dying
Lord.

St Catherine of Siena, St Catherine of Ricci, and
St Rose of Lima are exceptional, it is true, in the
intensity of their love. But their devotion to the
Passion makes them typical daughters of St Dominic.
St Dominic's[2] love for Christ crucified is too well
known to need emphasis. If it is objected that the

[1] *Vie*, by P. H. Bayonne, ch. viii, pp. 41-50.
[2] 1170-1221.

Preaching Friars became celebrated chiefly in the region of speculative philosophy, let it be remembered that their chief philosopher and theologian, St Thomas,[1] when asked the name of his Master, turned to his crucifix and replied simply: "There is my Master."

The preaching of the sons of St Dominic will teach the Christian world how to suffer with Christ, even more than how to reason.

" The Franciscans and Dominicans, by appealing continually to the heart, finally transformed the temperament of their hearers. They taught Europe to weep over the sacred wounds of our Lord."[2]

To the Dominican preachers we must add the Dominican mystics, and especially those belonging to the Rhenish provinces, such as Tauler and Suso.

The Blessed Henry Suso, writing in the troubled fourteenth century, seeks to revive religious fervour by opening his *Book of Eternal Wisdom* with an intensely realistic description of our Lord's sufferings. At the end of the volume are a hundred short meditations on the Passion, which are extraordinarily vivid and persuasive. He invokes our Lord in these words:

" Remember, O Lord, that terrible night in which thou didst so greatly suffer. Remember the sufferings of thy poor Mother when she saw them spit upon thy adorable face. Remember the moment when thy head was raised aloft on the tree of the cross, and the three hours' agony when thy thorn-crowned brow could find no place of rest. O adorable face polluted with spittle and blood, which even all the blood that flowed from thy veins could not wash away, grant that our eyes may see thee only on the cross, and our ears be deaf to earthly vanities, so that freed from the tyranny of the senses, we may care for nought save suffering and tears."

[1] 1225-1274. [2] E. Mâle, *op. cit.*, p. 383.

In another passage he addresses our Lady of Pity:
" O pure and tender Mother, remember the
infinite sorrow of heart which thou didst endure
at the first aspect of thy dear Child when thou didst
see him suspended in agony, and thou couldst not
come to his assistance; when thou didst gaze in
anguish of heart at thy beloved Son expiring before
thine eyes. Thou didst lament over him with great
lamentation; and he comforted thee very kindly.
How thy heart was torn by his cry of thirst, and his
abandonment by his Father! How thy body sank
exhausted on the ground, and thy tender mouth
did affectionately kiss his fallen blood! Remember,
O Refuge of sinners, the moment of thy Son's
death; how lovingly thine arms received his bruised
body, how lovingly thou didst kiss his bleeding
wounds, his pale and lifeless features! . . .   Let the
wounds of thy heart obtain for me a true repentance
of my sins and a tender compassion with thee in thy
sorrows."[1]

At nightfall, when the community were all asleep,
Blessed Henry Suso acted the drama of the Passion,
using the cloister and the monastery garden for the
different stations. He imagined one pillar in the
courtyard as the Garden of Olives, a corner of the
corridor as a part of the Prætorium, and another
pillar as a column in Pilate's house. Then in union
with our Lord he went from one spot to another
carrying a heavy cross. He spoke aloud, he wept and
he suffered. His Stations of the Cross came to an
end before the crucifix in the chapel. Then he went
silently back to his cell, imagining himself to accom-
pany our Lady after the burial, and " he saw her
covered with her Son's blood."

From the age of eighteen to forty his bodily
penances were appalling, but he imposed them on

---

[1] *Little Book of Eternal Wisdom*, pp. 157, 160.

himself. Then God himself took the scourge in his own hands.

"Till now it was thou who didst strike thyself, and at thy own bidding thou didst cease. It is my turn now, to try thee in my own way." And then followed a hundred different attacks upon his reputation: the loss of prestige, the suspicion of his brethren. God makes better crosses for us than we for ourselves.

One Candlemas Day Jesus said to him:

"Thou dost not know yet how to suffer; I will teach thee. When thou art in pain, do not be longing for the moment when it will cease, but on the contrary prepare thyself to bear patiently the next pang. Act like the young girl who is gathering roses. When she picks one flower from the bush, she is meaning to pass on and get others; thus when one trouble is over, prepare thyself for the next. Be of good courage, I shall be with thee, and I will help thee to overcome thy difficulties."

Our Lord interspersed his trials with ecstatic consolations. Blessed Henry Suso lived in a state of almost continual contemplation of Christ crucified, but it was less the cross of shame than the cross of glory; and as the monk contemplated his wounds and touched them, his heart overflowed with transports of love:

"Ah, my sweet Saviour, I seemed to desire to receive into my mouth one drop of blood from the open wounds of my Beloved. But, wonder of wonders, I have received from his heart, from his feet, from his hands, from all his tender wounds, not one or two drops, but the whole of his warm precious blood; it has flowed into my mouth and thence into my heart and soul."

In the year 1896 Preger discovered at Zurich an unknown work of Blessed Henry Suso entitled the *Little Book of Love*. In point of fact, there is no proof that this glowing and poetic composition is from his pen. But at any rate the inspiration and mode of expression are his. In the first chapter the soul is weeping over the bleeding features of our Lord:

" Come, my heart, keep silence and consider for one moment thy chosen Wisdom, thy Beloved. See how he is bathed in the blood-stream that gushes from all parts of his body under the violent blows of the scourges. See the scarlet rivulets that course over his delicate form and flow to the ground. Woe unto me for thy sake, O sweetest love of my soul ! "

In the second chapter he appropriates the feelings of our Lady of Sorrows at the hour of her Son's death as being most fitting when contemplating the Passion.

" O beauteous Flower, endowed with every grace, the blows of the hammers that nailed thy Son to the cross must have struck cruelly on thy heart. . . . O God ! If only I could have seen with my eyes my Saviour when he was taken down from the cross, and have watched the heartrending spectacle when his body rested inert on thy breast, O Mother . . . If only I could have heard thy bitter cry when thou didst find thyself gazing upon thy dead Child, and suddenly bereft of all consolation. At nightfall, when the beloved disciple led thee away from the tomb and through the city, what a piteous sight thou wast to the people that thronged the streets. They saw thy garments stained with the precious blood which fell upon thee all warm from the cross. The hardest hearts were moved to intense pity. . . ."

In the third part of the book the soul holds converse with her Spouse on Calvary, who has just been taken down from the cross. " I see my Beloved lying under a gnarled tree, covered with the wounds of love. . . . Although I am but an outcast, dust and refuse, I wish to speak to him, my tender Lord and shining Wisdom. . . . Tell me, my Beloved, how is it that thou hast left my soul to seek thee so zealously and so long and hast never shown thyself to me ? At night I sought thee among the pleasures of this world, and I found nought save that my heart was filled with bitterness."

And now that he has found his Saviour, he cries out to him with a wealth of imagery and tender expressions to show his pain.

Tauler, like Suso, was one of the great apostles of the interior life, and he writes very emphatically on the necessity of sacrifice. His teaching may be summed up in a few short extracts:

" Feelings of joy, pleasure, and satisfaction ought not to affect our interior life. Such sentiments should be merely transitory and cease when the act of which they are the effect is completed. Thou must no longer take pleasure in created things, thou must die to them . . . and put thyself above everything to which thou feelest an attraction."

Again, more briefly, he writes:

" Hasten to return within thyself and forget all that thou hast seen and heard. . . . Wherever thou hast denied thyself, there God will be found: when self is dead, God will take its place."

Tauler seems to have had a greater devotion to our Lord's interior sufferings than to his physical pains, and in particular to his abandonment by his Father, which certain modern writers have ventured to compare to the loss of the damned. Tauler's mystic mind, like that of Ruysbroeck in the green solitudes of Groenendael, found in his own spiritual desolation a faint glimpse of the agony of Christ when he cried: " My God, my God, why hast thou forsaken me ?" And this trend of mind had its effect upon the following century.

There still remains one other name to be mentioned

before this period is brought to a close; that of Ludolph the Carthusian, at the beginning of the fourteenth century. At a very early age he became a Dominican. Thirty years later a yearning for more complete solitude caused him to seek admission among the sons of St Bruno. He died in the Carthusian Monastery of Strasbourg in the year 1378.

It was there, although some say that it was at Mainz, that he composed his *Life of Christ*, which had an enormous success. A large number of copies were made, at first by hand, later in print, and many saints have been trained in the love of our suffering Lord by reading his impassioned words; for the finest passages are those which treat of the Passion. It was this book that St Teresa was reading in Spanish when she fell into an ecstasy, as she tells us in the thirty-eighth chapter of her *Life*. St Francis de Sales includes it among the small number of carefully selected books that he recommended to St Jeanne de Chantal.

Ludolph begins the fifty-eighth chapter with these words:

"The moment has come to treat of our Lord's Passion, which every Christian soul should recall to mind seven times a day." Then, having alluded to the saying of St Bernard: "The Passion should be the constant study of the devout Christian," he continues: "When the details of the Passion become the subject of our constant meditation, then we shall assuredly enter upon a new way of life. As we proceed, new aspects of the truth will be discovered, and will arouse in us lively sentiments of love and compassion. . . . Such was the experience of a certain holy nun, who was so moved by the thought of the Passion of Christ that she could never look at a crucifix without falling into an ecstasy."

It was from Ludolph that Gerson later borrowed the idea of dividing the Passion into seven parts, according to the canonical hours: " Compline, matins, prime, terce, sext, none and vespers, to correspond with the hours when our Lord was taken prisoner and so grievously tormented."[1]

It may be that this period and the influences we have described are responsible for certain ancient crucifixes which bear the following lines inscribed on the base:

> Dost thou doubt that I am love ?
> Pause then and gaze;
> Love itself is graven here
> On this form transfixed.

CHAPTER III

ST IGNATIUS LOYOLA AND ST TERESA OF JESUS— AFFECTIVE AND EFFECTIVE LOVE— THE " IMITATION "—ST FRANCIS DE SALES AND SOME MODERN EXAMPLES

I

THE Styrian poet Rosseger depicts for us a scene from the life of the beggar Wast.

" Wast had only one pleasure in life, and that was to pause beside every wayside Calvary. While the passers-by hurried unheeding, he would remain hour after hour in colloquy with the crucified Christ. Nor must it be imagined that he spoke of his own misfortunes, or of the rags he had been wearing for sixty years. No, the poor beggar was sympathising with our Lord. In words of infinite tenderness he

---

[1] This little book, *The Seven Hours of the Passion*, is an excellent volume for meditation. It was written in Latin originally by Gerson (the great chancellor of the university of Paris, in the time of St Jeanne d'Arc), who translated it into French at the request of his sister. Its style is simple, pious, and arresting.

said: 'This is a painful hour for thee, my Beloved. Thou needest patience to bear it, Jesus.' And he continued his words of sympathy until, as he believed, he had in some degree assuaged the divine agony.''

The mentality of Wast was that of the Middle Ages. In those days men paused when they saw a crucifix; or rather we should say that wherever possible they set up on high the sign of our redemption, and fell on their knees in adoration before it.

The Reformation overthrew the wayside crucifixes, and the spirit of the pagan Renaissance drove from men's minds all thought of the supernatural, so that little by little they forgot the cross of Christ. But it might be objected that the sentiments of pity which were so intensely vivid in the ages of faith were only a matter of sentiment, and therefore had no real importance. Sentiment, if you will, but the best of its kind. It was because St Veronica had a heart that was moved to sympathy that she merited the miracle of the imprint of the Holy Face upon her veil. For the same reason St Gertrude received the hidden stigmata, and St Francis of Assisi the visible wounds of the Crucified.

It is because of their loving dispositions that unknown humble souls have bravely borne indescribable mental and physical sufferings.

It is true that *affective* love, the form of love which is expressed by anguished cries and ardent transports, is not, perhaps, the highest and purest type of love, but must it therefore be disdained ?

No one would accuse a saint like Ignatius Loyola of laying too great a stress upon the affections, yet in a page or two of the *Exercises* there are no fewer than seven injunctions to the retreatant to become a partaker in the sorrow of Christ.

In the beginning of the meditation for the third week, in the third prelude, he is told: '' To ask for what I want, namely, to feel sorrow and affliction.''

In the fourth prelude he is told " to consider what Christ our Lord suffers, or wishes to suffer in his humanity . . . and here to begin with great force to strive to grieve, and bewail and lament." Here he uses three verbs: grieving, which implies the sighing of the heart; bewailing, the tears of the eyes; lamenting, words of sorrow; and he is told "to proceed in the same way with each mystery." The fifth point is to consider . . . how the Godhead allowed our Lord's human nature to suffer so cruelly.

In the third prelude of the second contemplation, the retreatant " asks for sorrow with Christ who is full of sorrow, and anguish with Christ in his anguish, and tears and interior pain for the great pain Christ has suffered for me."

The third note tells him " on waking and while rising and dressing, to grieve over the great sufferings and grief of Christ our Lord, and to endeavour not to admit joyful thoughts even though they are good and holy, but rather exciting myself to sorrow, pain, and anguish, recalling frequently to mind the troubles, labours and sorrows of Christ our Lord."[1]

St Angela Merici lived at the same time as St Ignatius, and was inspired by similar aims in founding the Ursuline Congregation, destined to combat the spread of heresy by means of the Christian school. She was remarkable for her burning love for Christ crucified. The Crusades had come to an end two centuries before, but she had a great desire to pray at the holy places where our Lord shed his blood. She set out in the year 1524, and curiously enough St Ignatius, at that time thirty-two years of age, was also at Jerusalem on a pilgrimage to the Holy Land. But when she arrived at the island of Crete, she suddenly lost her eyesight; so that it was only in imagination she was able to contemplate the scenes of our Lord's life, his birth,

[1] *Text of the Spiritual Exercises*, pp. 62, 64, and 65.

his agony and death and burial. On Calvary, she fastened herself in spirit to the cross by the three evangelical vows; then once more setting sail, she came to Crete again. On the island was a sanctuary containing a miraculous crucifix; she asked to be taken to the place, and there her sight was restored to her.

The disciples of St Ignatius of Loyola have always loved to share his ardent devotion to Christ crucified.

Peter Lefèvre, the first companion of the founder, gives us an example of this trait. He was travelling about Germany, fighting the new heresy, and one day he stopped at Spires to say Mass in the Church of Holy Cross.

" God inspired me," he writes, " with a great devotion for the cross in this church, and led me to venerate it and every other cross, and every sign of the cross that should be made throughout the world. . . . My wish was to have the image of the Crucified always in my mind." On another occasion, when he was near Mainz, he entered a church, also dedicated to Holy Cross, where a miraculous crucifix was preserved. " I was deeply moved," he says, " by the thought that so much goodness was ignored by men." He desired to make amends for the impious ingratitude of those heretics who destroyed the image of Christ crucified.

It is a remarkable fact that the most profound secrets of divine knowledge, such as revelations concerning the mystery of the Holy Trinity, and the dispensations of the supernatural order, were made known to St Ignatius when he was praying at the foot of the crucifix on the road to Barcelona, not far from the cave of Manresa. After his death, the crucifix was carried into the cave and fixed on to the rock, but later it was placed over the entrance door, where it now stands. When St Ignatius became the first general of his Order, he had always on his writing desk a crucifix, which, although it could hardly be considered a work of art, sufficed to arouse his devotion whenever he raised his eyes to it.

To remind himself of his crucified Saviour, he made use of the *Anima Christi*:

Soul of Christ, sanctify me.
Blood of Christ, inebriate me, etc.

St Francis Xavier in Goa and Singapore was the echo of his beloved founder. His well-known impassioned prayer has been turned into verse:

My God, I love thee, not because
I hope for heaven thereby,
    *   *   *   *   *
Thou, O my Jesus, thou didst me
Upon the cross embrace,
    *   *   *   *   *
And griefs and torments numberless,
And sweat of agony,
E'en death itself—and all for one
Who was thine enemy.

St Teresa is another contemporary of St Ignatius and St Francis Xavier. Knowing as we do the endowments of that loving soul, we shall expect to find in her a special and unique devotion to her suffering Master, and a love that vies in generosity with that of the Master himself.

" It happened one day," she says, " that when I was going into a little chapel, I saw a picture of our Lord covered with wounds, waiting to be exposed at the forthcoming festival. The picture gave such a touching representation of his sufferings for us, that the sight of our divine Master in such a state greatly upset me. I was overcome with such grief at the thought of the ingratitude with which I had repaid all this love, that it seemed as if my heart

would break. I fell on my knees close to my Lord,
and shed a torrent of tears, while begging him to
strengthen me so that I might never offend him
again."[1]

Her keen appreciation of the sufferings of her
adored Master wrung from her this sublime yet
baffling phrase:

" It seems to me that the sole object of existence
is suffering, and I ardently beg of God to send it me.
Sometimes from the depth of my heart I cry: ' Lord,
either to suffer or die, I ask nought beside.' "[2]

When a fortified town had to be besieged, it was
formerly the custom to throw logs of wood into the
surrounding moat, in order that the attacker might
be able to pass over this improvised bridge; and thus
did St Teresa dream of reaching her Lord. Between
her and his infinite and inaccessible love, which is the
centre of the citadel, a gulf yawns. How was it
possible to bridge it ?   Let crosses be thrown into the
chasm: little by little it will be filled up, so that it
will be possible to pass over.

She gave her daughters as her chief advice the
injunction " to cultivate unceasingly a great desire
to suffer for Jesus Christ on all and every occasion."

There are few writings to equal her *Prayer before a
Crucifix* in its tragic intensity and arresting appeal:
the compilers of spiritual anthologies may search
in vain, but they will never find anything more
sublime.

" Dost thou believe, O Eternal Lord, that I love
thee because of the promise of future rewards in thy
kingdom ?   Is it in the hope of winning the palm
and harp, and the wondrous delights of heaven ?
No, I love thee because of thy sufferings, and the
humiliations thou hast endured, thou who wast
bound and led away to suffer by thy executioners.
I love thee because of the cry that was wrung from

[1] *Life*, ch. ix.   [2] *Ibid.*, xl.

thee: 'My God, my God, why hast thou forsaken
me?' I love thee more for thy death and agony,
than for thy resurrection. For it seems to me, that
once thou hast returned to those azure heights, and
now that the whole universe lies at thy command,
thou wilt have less need of thy servant. But when
I am present at thy agony it is as if I were back in a
familiar country, for I have seen already the hill,
and the road washed with the purple of thy blood.
This Magdalen, thy saint, thy beloved, who is
standing weeping there, is it perhaps myself? For
my heart sorrows with her heart, the voice of her
lamentations rings in my ears, and my grief is so
intense and so terrible, that it seems as if two such
despairing persons could not exist. Her love was
not greater than mine. I know that she was a great
saint, and I am a poor sinner, whose acts are less
meritorious than hers, but she did not love thee
more. . . . Only once in her life did she fall weeping
on the blood-stained earth of Calvary, but how many
times have I done this? Almost every night the
sacrifice of Calvary has been renewed before me, so
that in spite of the lapse of centuries, that moment,
when in the darkness the Creator expired before
the eyes of all creation, is present to me in all its
reality. My eyes devour the cross of thy martyrdom,
whereon thy white form stands out, illumined by the
light of love, while the rest of my cell is plunged
in sepulchral darkness. Thou and I, Lord, and
no one else; close together, and yet so far apart,
for I am down under thy feet, and thou art hanging
nailed to those beams of cedar-wood, in the terrifying
darkness above. I am prostrate on my knees in
silence, but my whole frame is quivering in union
with the sufferings of thy body; the thorns on thy
brow pierce my temples, the nails of thy hands tear
my palms, my heart bleeds in sympathy with the
wound in thy side. And yet, although I am lying

in the dust, I feel that I also am up there on the cross, so closely am I united with thee."

There is an anguished appeal in these words, which seems to come from the bottom of her heart. Let those ingenuous persons who imagine that affective love is only a matter of words, and is of no importance, read these passages, and meditate upon them, and cease criticising what they do not understand. Mary herself, though she did not die a violent death, is nevertheless the Queen of Martyrs. Those who appear to undergo the greatest trials are not always the greatest sufferers.

II

Although affective love is one of our greatest treasures, it must not be imagined that it is all-sufficient. To be complete and sincere it must include effective love.

The best proof of love is to renounce one's life, or to devote it for the sake of the Beloved. "You say that you love me; then serve me." Compassion leads naturally to the desire to suffer with the sufferer, and the examples that have been mentioned show to what generous sacrifices it can lead.

The effort of will which is the accompaniment and sanction of loving aspiration is always the sign of the reality of love. Words of lyric fancy even when sincere may deceive; acts are never deceptive.

The story is told of a little boy, the child of a very poor family, who was sent at Christmas time to collect wood in the forest close by. His widowed mother, who was slowly dying, took the great-coat of her dead husband which supplemented the meagre coverings of her bed, and wrapped it round the child to keep him warm. The boy set off. His accustomed path lay past a wayside crucifix, and here, as usual, he paused to say an *Our Father*. Then suddenly he discovered something that he had not noticed before, that our Lord must be cold hanging nailed to that granite cross in this north wind. He took off his big coat, and climbing up to the pedestal of the cross, draped it over the figure of the Crucified. It was not right for him to be warmly dressed, when the gentle Saviour had no covering.

St Ignatius concludes his meditation on the sufferings of Christ with the words: "My heart is touched; what ought I to bear for Jesus Christ? Christ endured poverty, ought not I to embrace poverty? Christ was nailed to the cross, where are the nails of my calvary?"

The first Ignatius, the venerable Martyr of Antioch, uttered a similar cry when he was on the road to martyrdom: "My love is crucified," he said, and offered himself to be ground into wheat by the lions' teeth, so as to be a fit bread for his suffering Master. The originality of St Ignatius of Loyola certainly does not consist in his having taken little account of affective love, nor yet in his having invented effective love. The truth is that until his time it had not been thought necessary to insist on effective love, because it had been taken for granted that this would follow naturally from the affections of the heart. Ignatius was no less an enthusiastic lover than his predecessors, but his was an essentially active temperament, and he was therefore especially careful to make sure that man's will, which he knew to be weak and wavering, should persevere in its good intentions. He wanted to make men feel so that they might will; but, more than this, he wanted men to continue willing even when the feeling had passed away. Hence he stressed effective love. "Be precise as to what you intend to do." Impressions and sentiments pass away; resolutions must remain.

St Francis Xavier, in this matter, also a faithful

follower of his father Ignatius, was not satisfied with
merely loving the cross in his fervent prayers; he
seized the cross wherever he found it, and, never
content, longed always for a greater share of suffering. " More, still more, Lord !" he cried. And
when at the age of forty-three he was dying, stretched
out on the shore with his face turned towards
China, his last consolation was to kiss the cross of
the final sacrifice of his life.

The cross was so well known a weapon of those
who continued the Saint's work,[1] that some of the
Japanese, in order to hinder the missionaries from
landing, strewed the quay with crosses, and cried
out : " Do not come here, or you will tread under foot
the sign of your redemption."

It was not to be imagined that such a device would
drive them away. They landed and erected calvaries everywhere, until one day the governor of
the Province of Omura, infuriated with their zeal,
condemned them all to be fastened to crosses after
the example of their Master.

St Aloysius Gonzaga, too, was a martyr in his
daily life. He is usually represented in art as
clasping a crucifix to his breast, with instruments
of penance lying on his desk beside him.

The beatification of the Jesuit martyrs of Canada
in June, 1925, recalls to mind the heroic names of
Jogues, Lallemant, Lejeune, de Brébeuf and their
companions.

Father Jogues had his fingers eaten or cut off by
the savages. When, at the command of the sooth-
sayer, a woman cut off his thumb, he said: " I take
this thumb with my other hand, and present it to
thee, the one true living God, in memory of the
Holy Sacrifice which for seven years I have offered
up on the altars of thy Church."

[1] Among these were priests and religious of various
congregations and religious orders.

He returned to France in 1643, and in the following year went back to his beloved mission, with a dispensation from Urban VIII to allow him to say Mass in spite of the loss of some of his fingers. "It would be unjust," said the Pope, "for the martyr of Jesus Christ to be unable to drink the blood of Jesus Christ."

Jogues was martyred by blows from a hatchet on October 18, 1646. It is told of Lallemant that after his election, while he was making his retreat, he asked to be sent on the mission to the Huron and Iroquois Indians, so that he might suffer martyrdom. Another of his companions, Father Lejeune, writes: "Our lives must be thrown away, and all that we have, and we must be content with a large and weighty cross as our sole possession."

Brébeuf, the superior, had the thought of martyrdom perpetually before him. He had a vision of a great cross coming towards him from the Iroquois country, and thereupon he made a vow: "Not to avoid any opportunities that might offer of dying for Jesus Christ." His martyrdom was horrible: his whole body was lacerated, and an iron collar, made red-hot in the fire, was placed round his neck. When his wounds became too raw, they were tended in order that he might be fit to be tortured again. When at last he died, the chieftain of the tribe cut open his breast, and took out his heart, which he divided into little pieces and distributed to his fighting men, so that they might be filled with the indomitable spirit of the " white man."

Lejeune was right when he spoke of " a large and heavy cross as his sole possession."

But we cannot linger over these early days; there are other names to be mentioned, which brings us into touch with modern times, such as those of Father Olivaint, Father de Ravignan, and Father Ponlevoy. This last, in his commentary on the

Exercises, gives a beautiful meditation on the cross, which is entitled *To see, to hold, and to understand your crucifix*. They were words which became the inspiration of his daily life.

Father Ginhac had an extraordinary spirit of detachment; his face became so emaciated by his austere life that his English biographer remarks humorously, " that he appeared to be in dire need of a good dinner." Father Lenoir and Father Auffroy were curiously similar, and yet different. The former sacrificed himself heroically for his regiment, and met his death in the cornfields of Vardar, when he was carrying the Last Sacraments to the wounded. Father Auffroy asked leave of Pope Pius X to pray for martyrdom, and to organise among his companions a group who would prepare themselves for this end. Then there is Father William Doyle, that amazing Irishman, who, under the impulse of like aspirations, wrote down the following resolution during his noviciate: " Sweet Virgin Mary, as a preparation for the crown of martyrdom that thou wilt assuredly obtain for me, I purpose resolutely to begin a life of slow martyrdom, by unremitting labour and constant self-denial. . . . I wish to die a Jesuit and a martyr." The word martyr is marked with two stains of blood. His devotion for our Lord in his Passion was so real that one day when he was alone in a church, praying before a full-sized crucifix, he would not remain at our Lord's feet, but placed his two arms round his neck and remained in this attitude for some space of time. On another occasion he cut the name of Jesus upon his breast with a knife, and then branded it with a red-hot iron.

After a long day of work on the mission, he wrote:

" I made the Holy Hour prostrate upon the marble tiles, and by moving from one part to another every now and then, I was able to have the full benefit of the cold stone. Then for two hours I made the

Stations of the Cross, and took fourteen strokes of the discipline at each station. The remainder of the night I spent kneeling before the Tabernacle, with my arms outstretched for as long as I could bear the pain."

Affective and effective love were perfectly exemplified in the following resolutions, in which he bound himself:

1. Never to try to avoid suffering.
2. Of two courses, to choose the more painful.
3. Never to miss an opportunity of self-denial.
4. If possible never to omit any penances when indisposed.
5. To ask myself constantly: what further sacrifice can I make?

He was killed by a shell when he was carrying a wounded officer into the trenches.

Father Surin is another son of St Ignatius whom God endowed with a special gift of prayer; he declared unceasingly that self-sacrifice must come before anything else. He writes:

" I wish I could persuade those who desire to follow the interior life that the way leading to it does not consist in many meditations, nor in emotional feelings in our devotions, but in self-renunciation, both interior and exterior, in being ready for all forms of suffering, and in complete self-denial. If they faithfully practise this self-denial, which is the foundation and the crown of all virtues, they will find greater profit and make more progress than by any other exercise."[1]

It is difficult to make a selection among so many examples without being guilty of some serious omissions. Zealous lovers of Christ crucified are to be found among the various religious congregations, in fact, among all those men and women who are close followers of the doctrines and methods taught

[1] *Les Fondements de la Vie Spirituelle*, by Surin, p 103.

by St Ignatius. Their devotion to the Passion is expressed less by the fervour of their prayers, than by their zeal for the practical hidden Cross of their daily duties, and the perpetual acts of self-denial which it entails.

The life of St Madeleine Sophie Barat, whom the Church has recently canonised, is a typical instance. On April 6, 1849, she writes to Mother Roulière in these words:

" Turn once more to the study of our Lord in his sufferings, in his humiliations, and in his crucifixion. There we shall learn how to resign ourselves to be nothing, to be treated as of no importance."

To Mother Gazelli she writes on March 9, 1856:

" We do not meditate sufficiently upon our Lord in his Passion, and the awful humiliations that he suffered. It is because our meditations are so lacking in reality that they do not incite us to make more practical resolutions, and our slackness on the path of self-renunciation may be attributed in part to this negligence. . . . The more deeply we are impressed with the necessity of identifying ourselves with Christ crucified, the more ready shall we be to imitate him; for courage springs from this habitual thought."

Again she said: " We meditate upon the Passion in a superficial manner; we are sorry for his sufferings, and that is all. But do we put it into practice, do we imitate him ? . . ."[1]

Philippe Duchesne, the foundress of the first house of the Sacred Heart in America, was a worthy successor of her mother. She was called the St Francis Xavier of the Order, for she always slept on the bare boards, covered with an old black cloth as her sole protection against the cold.

The history of the Congregation of the Sacred

[1] *St Madeleine Sophie Barat*, by Brou, pp. 215-220.

Heart[1] tells us that others have followed in the footsteps of these noble examples, and the majority of religious institutions can boast of similar heroic souls.

The teaching of St Teresa is identical with that of St Ignatius. " The essential point," she says, " is not to think a great deal, but to love greatly. And loving does not consist in wonderful emotions, but in the firm resolve to please God in all things." It will be seen further on in this volume how faithfully and even heroically the daughters of St Teresa preserved the tradition of their foundress.

The same idea is to be found in the books of St John of the Cross and the other masters of the spiritual life.

" He who is willing to suffer for God shows clearly that he has given himself to God, and loves him." On the contrary, " he who seeks a pleasant and easy life, and is afraid to imitate Jesus Christ, is not, in my opinion, a saintly man." And again: " Have a great desire to be made like unto this great God, your humble and crucified Lord, and to suffer with him. For of what use is this life if it be not spent in imitating him ?"

His life gives an added weight to his words. In addition to a malady that tormented him, in addition to interior sufferings, he was subjected to the suspicion of his superiors, the most terrible trial that a religious can have to bear. He was persecuted and imprisoned. He accepted everything with a smile. " If you have a real desire to find and possess Jesus Christ," he writes, " do not attempt to seek him without the Cross."

He had a burning desire to find and to possess our Lord. His biographers tell us that he often heard a voice saying to him: " Thou shalt be a martyr." God asked of him not the martyrdom of the body,

---

[1] *Religieuses du Sacré Cœur*, 1925.

but a complete and generous sacrifice of self in the details of daily life. Nor could there have been any better method of preparing him for the gifts of contemplation which God granted to him and which he so graphically describes than this hourly martyrdom undergone in perfect correspondence with grace.

III

The enemies of the Church and the profane do not understand the facts that we have related. This religion stained with blood revolts them; they will not accept it.

It is evident that, while every Christian is bound to have the spirit of self-sacrifice, there is still room for distinction between keeping the commandments, observing counsels of perfection, and finally those special acts of heroic devotion upon which, in this work, we have been laying such emphasis. We do not mean to propose these last for universal imitation. Our purpose is rather to show of what wonders the human heart is capable under the impulse of charity.

What is required of every Christian is to take up the cross which is involved in the faithful observance of the commandments. But for some this will not be sufficient; in every campaign there are volunteers for the posts of danger.

It is to be noted that we may consider the cross in two ways. We may point to the hard knobs on it, or we may contemplate Christ as he hangs upon it. In other words, some like to present the religion of Christ as one which can be admirably adapted to our human nature, while others emphasise the points where man's nature will have to suffer violence.

The ascetic practices of the early ages may seem to us uncouth and terrible. The hermits and solitaries were not self-indulgent. When the young

nobles came to St Bernard and asked to be shown
the way to God, he did not mind what means he used
to discipline them, to curb their pride, and to induce
them to give up their love of comfort.

There are some who, while they keep the fundamental austerity of such practices, nevertheless
adopt a somewhat different method. This may be
seen in the *Imitation*, where no word occurs more
frequently than Peace. There is also frequent
mention of the cross and of the Passion, but the
urgent call to the practice of self-denial is so closely
allied to the thought of the peace that it will bring
to the soul that it is impossible to say on which
of the two ideas the author wishes to lay the greater
emphasis. For example, he says: " Rest on the
Passion of Christ, and willingly dwell in his sacred
wounds. For if thou fly devoutly to the wounds
and precious stigmata of Jesus, thou shalt find
great comfort in tribulation."[1] Here it is the
thought of the Passion that is to mitigate our own
suffering, rather than our suffering that is to console
Christ in his Passion.

Another characteristic of this school is that they
endeavour to smooth over any detail of Christian
mortification that may give offence, with the object
of making it more universally acceptable. They lay
stress upon acts of humility in daily life, and urge
the necessity of trying to preserve a tranquil mind
while practising acts of self-denial. All this does
not imply a lessening of the spirit of mortification.
It means that the soul, while offering itself whole-
heartedly, also takes into consideration the human
factors which enter into the problem. There is the
question of time; and mortification is slow work.
The frailty of human nature must not be forgotten.
Sanctity does not consist in a triumphal march from
one victory to another, but in winning back lost

[1] *Imitation*, Bk. II, ch. i.

ground. Finally, there are many varieties of temperaments, and the same quota of self-denial cannot be required of them all.

Fundamentally all ascetics are agreed upon the necessity of mortification, but some of them go ahead without heeding these details, while others, more solicitous for the possible obstacles that may arise from human nature, in order to overcome them, insist upon certain distinctions which they consider of importance.

" It is good to mortify the flesh," says St Francis de Sales (1567-1622), the writer who best exemplifies this method; " but above all, we must purify our affections and refresh our hearts.   God tells us ' to beat, break and melt our hearts, for his anger is aroused against them.'   This is what we can do by little acts of mortification, often repeated and faithfully carried out: meekly suffering a little rebuff; obeying when it is very distasteful to do so; not complaining when we have a good reason for doing so; putting up with the faults of those with whom we live.   It is by occasions such as these that the heart must be broken and bruised.   We must make a continual sacrifice of our own will, tastes and natural inclinations, and give to God these signs of our love and fidelity."

St Jeanne de Chantal repeats much the same advice.

" The secret of the spiritual life is to keep ourselves close to God, and to walk in the continual presence of his divine Majesty, but by faith, and not by sentiment.   This presence of God within us must be accompanied by the death of self.   These two practices cannot be separated.   To walk in the presence of God is to walk in the path of his good pleasure, and not according to the flesh, or human understanding, or self-love; not in self-esteem or attachment to our own judgement and will, but

according to the divine will; to lose our own interests,
and self-will in the will of God."

The final aim of all penance is our life in God;
on this our author always insists.

" The soul that desires God to live in her, leaves
nothing unmortified in herself which may be displeasing to the divine eyes.   Her longing for him
is so great that she readily does violence to herself
so as to die to herself, that God may live eternally
in her."

In another passage we find the same idea: " Your
acts of violence against self must be gentle but also
firm.   They must cause you to labour unremittingly
in a faithful and loving spirit because you are striving
for God and eternity.   Boldly slay the enemy, for by
his death you will gain the peace and life of your
soul."

In conclusion, a quotation from St Francis de
Sales shall be given, which might equally be from
the pen of his spiritual daughter, and therefore
furnishes the key to their common position.

" I advise the practice of loving mental prayer,
and particularly meditation upon the life and Passion
of our Lord.   By looking often at him in your meditation, your soul will become filled by him, you will
think, love and act like him."

There is no foundation for the reproach that
Christianity is a religion of suffering: Christ did not
create pain.   The blame must be laid upon sin.
Our Lord came to pay the price of sin by his sufferings.   Probably the fact of his having chosen this
method of redeeming mankind confuses our minds.
But once the true signification is made clear, what
merciful loving-kindness it reveals !   The *Imitation*
is far-seeing when it tells the afflicted soul to turn to
the Cross, like the children of Israel in the desert who
were told to lift their eyes to the brazen serpent and
thus gained relief from their pains.

Only a superficially minded person can imagine sacrifice to be a degradation of human nature.

Sacrifice ennobles man, it does not degrade him. It destroys everything that hinders his upward progression; herein lies its divine function. The practice of true Christianity implies a life of complete submission to the will of God, instead of an existence governed by our own whims and fancies. This is the meaning of the expression: " To me to live is Christ."

In this way the words of our Lord: " My meat is to do the will of him that sent me,"[1] will be put into practice at every moment of our lives. The substitution of Christ for self will not reduce our activity, but increase it to infinitude.

Although compassionate love under the different forms which have been mentioned seem to have been the predominant note in medieval piety, it must not therefore be imagined that the " folly of the Cross " in other ages has been lacking in this trait.

It may be seen, for example, in the notes of the penitent Louise de la Vallière. Her one thought, in her Carmelite convent in the rue St Jacques, was to meditate upon Christ crucified and to serve him. " When I am not suffering I am tranquil, but when I suffer I am beside myself with joy," Father Eudes writes in his book, *The Profession of Love for the Cross*. " Jesus, my crucified Love, I adore thee in all thy sufferings. I ask pardon for all wherein I have been wanting during the trials which thou hast seen fit to send me until now. I desire the spirit of the Cross so that, imbued with this and with the love of the whole of heaven and earth, I may embrace generously all the crosses of body and soul that may be sent for love of thee. I declare my desire to glory in thy cross. May it be my treasure, so that I may find my contentment in humiliations, privations, and

[1] St John vi.

sufferings, and say with St Paul: ' God forbid that I should glory, save in the cross of our Lord Jesus Christ.' "[1]

In the eighteenth century, even in royal circles, there were souls who were attracted by the sufferings of Christ crucified. Marie Leczinska, the king's wife, is well known for her many virtues, and in particular for her love of the Sacred Heart. On the door of the tabernacle in her chapel at Chambord she had two crowns painted, the lower a crown of thorns, and above it a crown of glory, and the words: "One or the other." Louise de France, the daughter of Louis XV, became a Carmelite, and her life[2] should be read by all. Madame Elizabeth, sister of Louis XVI, prepared herself for her imprisonment in the Temple, and her death on the guillotine, by her assiduous meditations on the cross.

At the present day the spirit of compassion with our Lord in his sufferings has given rise, among other pious activities, to the devotion to the Holy Face, of which we shall speak later on. The same acts of generosity, the same ejaculations are aroused now as in the past, by the vision of Christ crucified which is ever the same. " To look at the cross is not enough," cried Thérèse Durnerin, the foundress of the Congregation of the *Amis des Pauvres*. "We must do more, we must be nailed to the wood of the cross itself."[3]

A little girl of seven, who had just undergone a most painful operation in the ear, was asked if she had suffered much. She replied: " Yes, but I thought of how Jesus suffered much more on the cross, and so I did not cry out aloud."

Marie Dominic Moes, foundress of the Dominican

[1] Gal. vi 14.—*Abrégé du Royaume de Dieu*, by Granger, p. 520.
[2] Edition *Les Saints*, by G. de Grandmaison.
[3] *Vie*, by Hamez, p. 386.

Convent of Luxembourg, who lived at the time of Lacordaire, offered herself as a victim in order to obtain from God the restoration of the Dominican Order in France. According to her revelations, our Lord is specially pleased with these proofs of compassionate love which throughout the ages are offered to him by souls of the type of St Veronica.

" I am pleased to find this compassion in thee, for among the majority I meet with nothing but hatred and scorn. They pass me by as if I had done nothing for them."[1]

This too rapid survey brings us to the great saint of France, who, in the seventeenth century, did so much to give a fresh interpretation to the love of Christ crucified. With St Margaret Mary, emphasis is laid upon compensation: the offering of a great love to counterbalance the weight of the sins of mankind.

This characteristic does not lessen her ardent desire to compassionate our Lord; it rather intensifies it.

[1] *Les Divines Paroles*, by Saudreau, p. 119.

PART II

COMPENSATION

CHAPTER I

ST MARGARET MARY AND THE SANCTITY OF JUSTICE

IN the first ages of Christianity, at the time of the great controversies, the faith had to be expounded and defended by the aid of philosophy. But when the great heresies came to an end, philosophy began to give way to contemplation.

To contemplate a thing means to gaze upon it, and to gaze for a prolonged space of time. Our attention is first drawn to our Lord in his human life, as seen from the exterior. And in his human life the most striking event in our eyes is his elevation upon the cross. Then through the wound in his side we penetrate within to his soul, and thus endeavour to gain a better understanding of the motives for such a sacrifice.

In other words, from contemplation we pass on to philosophise again.

To look is not sufficient: we want to go deeper. And the result of this investigation is that Christian piety takes the form of making compensation to a greater degree than before. Our Lord himself asked for this compensating love from her whom he was about to take as his special confidant in the revelations of his Sacred Heart. Let us therefore invoke the assistance of St Margaret Mary. She will teach us how to continue the love of compassion, while initiating us into the secrets of " compensation."

Even before her entry into the religious life, she had only one desire: to be conformed to the suffering life of our Lord. Throwing herself at the foot of her crucifix, she cried: "O my beloved Lord, how happy I should be if thou wouldst impress upon me the image of thy sufferings."

As soon as she arrived at the convent, our Lord made her understand that her vocation was to obtain the salvation of sinners. But how was this possible for a contemplative? It could be done in this way: "By appeasing his offended justice, and that can be done only by the sacrifice of a victim."

All through her life the Saint had this twofold objective in view: to make reparation for sinners, and to become like unto him whom she loved.

"My daughter, wilt thou not give me thy heart, where my love, which all the world despises, may find rest?"

On another occasion he said to her:

"See the ill-treatment that I suffer from this soul that has just received me. I desire . . . thee to prostrate thyself at my feet after thou hast received me, to make honourable amends to my heart, and offer to my Father the blood-stained sacrifice of the cross for this intention, together with thy whole self. . . ."

Our Lord enlightened her before her profession as to what he desired of her:

"Remember that it is a crucified Lord whom thou desirest as thy spouse; therefore in order to become like unto him, thou must bid farewell to all earthly pleasures, for everything thou hast shall be marked with the Cross."

During her retreat she received fuller inspirations, and her attraction for the cross increased. She could not bear the thought of "living a moment without suffering."

" See the wound in my side where thou shalt find
thy perpetual abode: henceforward be deaf, dumb,
blind, and insensible to all earthly things."

She signed the words of her religious profession
with her blood, and wrote: " Margaret Mary dead
to the world." At the foot of the page she added
three times the words: " All God, none of myself; all
God's, nothing mine; all for God, nothing for myself."

Shortly after our Lord revealed to her the two
aspects of holiness—" the sanctity of justice"
and " the sanctity of love"; which from that time
onward became two alternating inspirations in the life
of the great contemplative. At one moment the
thought of his outraged justice and of the innumerable sins that are committed overwhelmed and
crushed her; at another the thought of his burning
love and inexhaustible mercy transported her with
joy.

One day, in the year 1673, while she was contemplating our Lord in Gethsemane, and her mind was
full of the thought of his outraged justice, our
Lord said to her:

" It was here that my interior sufferings were
more intense than during all the rest of my Passion,
for I saw myself forsaken completely by heaven and
earth, and weighted down by the sins of mankind. . . .
My justice is angered, I am ready to punish with
manifest chastisements those who sin in secret,
unless they do penance."

What was she to do ? Our Lord told her to
make an offering of herself, and to offer him to the
Father for the redemption of the world, " making
a continual oblation of me to my Father as a victim
of love immolated for sin; thus placing me as a
rampart between his justice and the sinner, so as to
obtain mercy." Later on she says: " Our Lord is
weary of waiting . . . my chosen people persecute
me in secret."

Our Lord meant by " my chosen people " those who are specially dedicated to God. And alas! how many there are among those who should be the flower of the Christian religion who fall away and offend God!

" He showed me his loving heart, torn and pierced with wounds. ' See,' he said, ' the wounds I receive from my chosen people. Others are content to strike my body, but these attack my heart. . . . My love will give way before my just wrath, and I will chastise them. . . . They are religious only in name.' "

The Saint adds:

" During this time I besought God unceasingly to give the grace of a true conversion to those who had incurred his just wrath. I offered to him the merits of our Lord in satisfaction for the offences committed against him; I declared that I was ready to suffer all the pains which he saw fit to send me . . . rather than see the souls which had cost him so dear perish eternally."

Another day she writes:

" After Holy Communion, he showed me a rough crown composed of nineteen very sharp thorns which were piercing his head. . . . He told me that he had come to look for me, in order that I might pull out these thorns which had been driven in by a faithless spouse." This person had sinned through pride. Our Lord asked, therefore, for acts of humility in reparation.

" After five days, he showed me three thorns which had been taken out, giving him great relief; the others remained for a long time." Our Lord specially chose St Margaret Mary to make acts of compensation for the sins of these chosen souls. And she knew well, this valiant saint, what it would cost her. She tells us in her autobiography:

" My Sovereign Lord told me that when he was

about to abandon someone for whom he wished
me to suffer, he would put me into the state of
a damned soul, and cause me to feel the desolation
that such a soul would experience at the hour of
death. I have never known anything more terrible;
there are no words to express it. One day, when I
was sitting alone working, I suddenly saw before me
a nun who was still alive, and I heard a voice saying
to me: 'See this nun who is a religious only in name.
I am ready to vomit her out of my heart, and to
abandon her to herself. . . .' I offered myself to
the divine Justice to suffer all that he wished, so that
he might not forsake her. Then it seemed to me that
his just wrath was turned upon me, and I was in
a state of terrible anguish and desolation." Our
Lord did not force upon her this rôle of making
compensation. He asked her to accept it of her own
free will.

"My daughter, art thou willing to give me thy
heart as a place of rest for my outraged love which
is scorned by the whole world? . . . I have
chosen thee to offer a burnt-offering to my eternal
Father to appease his justice and render to him
infinite glory. And this thou wilt do by the oblation
thou wilt make of me with these sacrifices, offering
with them thy whole self in my honour."

It may be pointed out that this method of making
compensation involves an important truth of Catholic
doctrine. The one person in the whole world who
can offer adequate reparation to the Father is Jesus
Christ. Therefore it is he who must be offered to the
Father; and it is in our power to do so, for in baptism
we received this priestly power proper to every
Christian, which St Peter calls " a royal priesthood."
We have no right to stand aloof from this sacrifice;
we should place ourselves beside our Lord on the
sacrificial altar. Everyone who understands the
significance of a true life in Christ will see the

necessity of so doing. Frequently our Lord would
lay stress upon his sufferings when speaking to his
servant. "See, my daughter, the ill-treatment which
I am suffering from this soul that has just received
me. . . . I desire . . . thee, whenever thou receivest me, to prostrate thyself at my feet, to make
amends to my Sacred Heart; to offer the bloody sacrifice of the cross to the Father for this same object,
together with thy whole self, to do me homage and to
repair the insults that I suffer in my Sacred Heart.
Not that this person is in sin, but the inclination to
sin has not been driven out of his heart, which I abhor
more even than the sin itself."

Sometimes the Saint emphasised the offering that
she was making of our Lord:

" My God, I offer thee thy beloved Son. . . ."

At other times the stress was on her offering of
her whole being:

" I placed myself at his feet as a living sacrifice,
having no desire but to be offered up and immolated
. . . ; my greatest satisfaction was to become like
unto my crucified Spouse."

St Francis de Sales in a celebrated vision reminded
her of the duty of making amends for the sins of
others. " As the general slackness which creatures
have allowed to slip into their lives is the cause of
these failings (in humility and charity) and of many
others, reparation must be made for these faults
by a spirit of loving severity and continual watchful-
ness. . . . I shall come on my feast day and choose
out my true daughters . . . and offer them to the
divine Majesty . . . to make amends for those who
are imperfect."

For, alas! these imperfect souls were not lacking.

" I saw our Lord with a heavy burden, and he said
to me: ' Art thou willing to bear the weight of my
outraged justice ? I am on the point of letting it
fall upon this religious here; and he showed her to

me.   When I rose from my knees I found myself
weighted down with such a load that I could not
move." And for some time after this the Saint
suffered from a painful malady.

Our Lord called upon her to make reparation for all
kinds of sins and failings.   He revealed to her how
an unworthy Communion grieved him.   "See how
these sinners treat me."   And these words, together
with the vision of his sufferings which accompanied
them, caused her indescribable suffering.

" I saw him in the heart of one who was resisting
his love; his hands were pressed against his ears, his
eyes were closed, and he said: ' I will no more listen
to what he is saying to me, nor will I look upon his
misery lest my heart should be moved to compassion.' "

Our Lord suggested to her a pious practice for the
conversion of hardened sinners.   Every Friday she
was to prostrate herself thirty-three times in adoration at the foot of the cross.   Frequently the Master
complained of coldness, and asked her to show him
a little love.   "Thou at least."   And to make her
less incapable of supplying his needs, he imparted
to her a spark of his divine love, and urged her to go
to Holy Communion as often as she could.

Among other practices which he asked her to
adopt, the Holy Cross merits special mention.   The
object of this devotion is twofold.   " It seeks to
appease the divine wrath by pleading for mercy
upon sinners, and also in some manner to relieve
the bitterness which I suffer from the abandonment
of my chosen disciples."

In her autobiography she tells us that our Lord
said to her:

" Every Thursday night to Friday morning I
will cause thee to share in the mortal sorrow which
I chose to experience in the Garden of Olives. . . .
And in order that thou mayest bear me company

in the prayer which I humbly offered to my Father
in my agony at that time, thou shalt rise between
eleven o'clock and midnight, and for the space of an
hour lie prostrate with me, thy face to the ground
. . . and during that hour thou shalt do what I
shall show thee. . . ."[1]

St Margaret Mary declares that the greatest graces
of God were vouchsafed to her either after Holy
Communion or during the Holy Hour. She makes
special allusion to those night watches when our
agonising Saviour made her a participant in the
mortal anguish of Gethsemane. He told her: "I
suffered there more than in all the rest of my Passion
because I saw myself completely forsaken by heaven
and earth and weighted down by the sins of mankind. I stood confronted by the holiness of God,
who, heeding not my innocence, smote me in his
anger, and made me drink to the dregs the chalice
of his bitterness and just indignation, as if he had
forgotten the name of Father and desired only to
sacrifice me to his just wrath. There is no created
being who can realise the terrible sufferings which I
then experienced."

The vision of this awful mystery which in some
fashion was revealed to the Saint caused her intense
sorrow. These revelations of the agony of Gethsemane were followed by a participation in the
torments of the crucifixion.

The Holy Trinity appeared to her and made her
the gift of the cross. Then our Lord came and
promised her "a hunger which nothing can satisfy,
an unquenchable thirst, and a zeal which cannot be
appeased," a continual longing for suffering in
union with the burning desire for suffering of our
Redeemer.

Jesus showed her two pictures. One represented
our Lord in a triumphant state; the other showed a

---

[1] *Autobiography*, ii, p. 72.

bleeding, suffering Christ. And without a moment's hesitation she chose the picture of the crucifixion.

These are no mere words. For a time she was sent into the infirmary, and the heroic acts of mortification to which her zeal for self-sacrifice led her may readily be conjectured. Our Lord enjoined her to study the crucifix " so as to become a living image of her crucified love . . . and when her likeness has become conformable to his own, he will fasten her to the cross."

She aimed at the most perfect likeness possible, " having no more burning desire than to make herself a faithful and perfect copy of her crucified Jesus."

Our Lord was constantly showing her the vileness and frailty of humanity. On November 20, 1677, he asked her to offer herself as a victim to compensate for the lukewarmness of mankind as a whole, and in particular for a certain religious community whose fervour had become lukewarm.

" I desire thee to make amends for their ingratitude through the merits of my Sacred Heart. I wish to give thee my heart; but first thou must become its sacrificial victim, so that by means of my Sacred Heart thou mayest stay the hand of chastisement which the Father in his divine justice is about to let fall upon this religious community, which, in his wrath, he wishes to reprove and punish."

This was one of the rare occasions on which, since our Lord had called her to adopt the practice of making special reparation, she became alarmed. The thought of God's justice and the need of making amends frightened her, and she tried to hide herself. " I had not the courage to sacrifice myself," she humbly confesses. But it was only for a moment. Our Lord soon calmed her fears and promised her his help. If she would consent to aid him, he would come and assist her.

5

It was the time of the annual retreat, in the year 1678. Our Saviour spoke plainly to her in these words:

" I desire thy heart to be my refuge, where I may retire and take my pleasure when sinners persecute me and turn me out of their hearts. When I make known to thee that the divine Justice is angry with them, thou shalt come and receive me in Holy Communion. Then having placed me on the throne of thy heart, thou shalt adore me, and, prostrating thyself at my feet, offer me to my eternal Father as I shall show thee, to appease his just wrath and move him to have mercy and pardon them. When I have made my will known, thou wilt make no resistance to it. . . . Thou art the victim of my Heart and must be ready to be a sacrifice of love."

From that day she resolved upon making a complete gift of herself to the Sacred Heart. She wrote the name of Jesus with a knife upon her breast and sealed the gift with her blood.

She had a burning desire to unite herself with our Lord in his thirst on the cross, and for fifty days remained without drinking.

Henceforth she was consumed by two great longings—to go to Holy Communion, and to suffer. During the retreat of 1679 she burnt afresh the name of Jesus on her chest with a lighted candle.

Our Lord often reminded her of her rôle of victim, but more especially at times when sins were more frequent. After Holy Communion he said to her: " I have come that thou mayest make reparation for the injuries which I have received from these lukewarm nuns who dishonour me in the Blessed Sacrament. This soul that I have given thee, thou shalt offer to God my Father, to turn away the chastisement which those unfaithful souls have merited. By my spirit thou shalt make sincere acts of adoration for those hypocrites who adore me without meaning what they say. This thou shalt do for my chosen people. It was for this end that I made thee this great gift."

During the carnival of 1682, after Holy Communion, our Lord revealed himself as the *Ecce Homo*, bearing his cross, and covered with wounds so that his precious Blood was flowing from all sides. "Is there no one," he cried, "who will have pity, and sympathise with me and share in my grief, at this time above all when sinners have reduced me to such a pitiable condition?" St Margaret Mary offered herself unconditionally. "Then I found myself burdened with a heavy cross bristling with sharp nails. I began to realise more fully the malice of sin. . . . He showed me . . . that I had to be fastened to the cross with him . . . by sharing in his sufferings, the scorn, ignominy and other indignities that he had undergone. This he brought about by sending me a terrible illness."

Her notes written at the time of the jubilee of Autun, in the month of May, tell us of a similar revelation, and on this occasion, as frequently before, she was urged to make intercession for those chosen souls who neglect him:

" He showed me that his justice was more offended by his own chosen people who had rebelled against him than by the heathen. . . . I had to weep and sigh continually because his blood was shed in vain for so many souls. . . . Woe unto those who have not washed their sins away in these living waters."

Then follows the phrase:

" One just man can obtain pardon for a thousand evildoers."

Our Lord made her share both in the agony and in the crucifixion. Her part in the crown of thorns consisted in terrible headaches. She wrote to Mother de Saumaise:

" This suffering is the more precious to me inas-

much as it is continual and often prevents me
sleeping, so that I cannot even remain in bed. I
pass wonderful nights in company with Jesus suffering for love of us." Her favourite mystery of the
Passion, so she tells Sister Le Barge, was our Lord's
silence. She loved " to keep silence as he did, in
times of humiliation or suffering."

She was quite insatiable. It was not merely
this or that part of her body that she offered to
satisfy his justice, but her whole self.

During her retreat of 1684, she tells us, " our Lord
made me understand that he destined me to render
continual homage to him as host and victim in the
Blessed Sacrament. I was to make the sacrifice of
my whole self by continual acts of love, adoration,
and self-immolation in union with the death of Christ
on the altar in the Holy Eucharist, taking him as
my model in the practice of my vows."

The word " host," which has been misused to a
certain extent, is here given a deep significance.

" My longing to suffer became so great that I
should have liked every instrument of torture to be
used for my martyrdom." She declared to Father
Rolin, the former superior of the Jesuit house at
Paray-le-Monial, that the sorrows of our Lord's
Sacred Heart had made such a deep impression upon
her, " that only one thing is possible to me, to offer
myself as a victim to be immolated to his justice."

On her feast day, January 29, 1687, the saintly
Founder of her Order told her " that a true daughter
of the Visitation should be a living victim."

St Margaret Mary was a daughter of the Visitation
in the full sense of the term.

CHAPTER II

ST MARGARET MARY AND THE SANCTITY OF LOVE

At the beginning of her religious life, St Margaret Mary had an enormous cross presented to her, of which she could not see the end. It was covered with flowers; but she learned that " gradually the flowers would fall and only the thorns remain."

The Saint's description of these thorns is so realistic that we pity her, and are tempted to say to our Lord: " This is too much, spare her ! Art thou an executioner ?" Our Lord certainly is not an executioner. He is love itself, and all his appeals to us to suffer with him are in reality only demands for our love.

If he were to offer us only the flowers, instinctively we should look for the thorns as a means of proving our love. Therefore even if the sanctity of justice did not demand reparation, love would always urge the soul to self-immolation. The desire to make reparation for insults committed against the majesty of God is a great incentive. But to make amends because the love of God is scorned is an even stronger motive. There is no sacrifice which the soul is not ready to accept, at times even to seek, in order to satisfy this love.

"My daughter, art thou willing to give me thy heart as a resting-place for my sorrowful heart when all the world despises my love ?" St Margaret Mary realised that great opportunities for self-sacrifice are rare. Our Lord demands renunciation for his sake in all the little opportunities which his Providence prepares; readiness to accept any circumstances that may arise: difficulties due to health, the observance of the rule, obedience to superiors. We have written of her vow of perfection elsewhere.[1]

[1] *Christ in His Brethren*, Bk. III, ch. viii, pp. 201-2.

She writes to Mother de Saumaise:

" If you only knew how he (our Lord) urges me to love him and to make some return for his life of suffering, not by enduring extraordinary trials, but by remaining in a continual state of sacrifice! To accomplish this he himself provides the means, for every action that I perform is a fresh torment owing to the distaste which he gives me the grace to experience."

In another letter addressed to the same correspondent, she makes it clear that " the love of the cross is pure love." Then she boldly exhorts her former superior to make the full sacrifice of her heart to the sovereign King, " so that all that you do is done out of pure love, and for no other motive than to procure for him all the honour and glory that is in your power."

She declared to another Superior, Mother Greyfie, that she preferred the cross, with the possibility of being able to extend the reign of the Sacred Heart, to the joy of the seraphim.

" I can think of nothing that would make the days of our life pass so peacefully," she writes to Sister le Barge, " as to be always suffering out of love. Let us then suffer in this way, and count those moments lost that are passed without pain."

On another occasion she says to her:

" We must not lose a moment of suffering because we cannot love without pain. . . ." In another passage, she explains what she means by suffering; for although for her own part she was ready to take the biggest share, she knew how to maintain her Sisters in the discreet and prudent way.

" It is not necessary to ask for suffering. It is more perfect to ask nothing and refuse nothing, but to abandon ourselves to pure love so that he may crucify and destroy self as he sees best."

She remarks naïvely that it is not too much to love

Love himself with all our powers of affection. How foolish are those who waste their treasure by dispersing their love upon worthless objects !

" The heart is so small that it cannot hold two objects of our affection, and having been made for divine love, it can have no rest when its affections are divided." When the thought of hell comes into her mind, it is especially abhorrent to her because in hell there is no charity:

" Is it reasonable to imagine that there is any place in the world where our Lord is not loved ?"

Her rule of life is to love, and to show her love by the utmost generosity.

" I do not know how a spouse of Christ crucified can dislike the cross and flee from it, for by so doing she is turning her back upon him who bore it for love of us. . . . He told me that as often as I came into touch with the cross, and lovingly placed it in my heart, I should receive him and should feel his presence in my heart." Thus did our Lord reward her by the generous outpouring of his tender love.

The first great favour which he granted her was the privilege of resting on his Sacred Heart, like the apostle St John, and this caused an interior wound which the Saint felt every Friday.

Our Lord says to her:

" My heart is so touched by thy desires that even if I had not already instituted the Sacrament of my love I should do so now, so as to become thy food."

He invites her " to enter into his heart." She explains to Mother de Saumaise how our Lord made this known to her on the feast of the Ascension, 1680:

" I have chosen thy soul to be my resting-place on earth; and thy heart will be a throne of delight for my divine love."

Again she speaks of this:

" One Friday he placed my mouth to the wound of his sacred side, and held me there close pressed against it in indescribable transports of delight for the space of three or four hours."

She tells Sister le Barge, her beloved confidante, naïvely:

" Now we must always nestle in this adorable Heart, and never leave it whatever happens."

Our Lord remained continually present with her. She never lost sight of him, she told Father Rolin. The good Master went so far as to make her, so to speak, the mistress of the riches of his Heart.

" In return for thy life as victim, thou shalt possess the treasures of my Heart as I promised thee, and I permit thee to bestow them as thou wishest upon those persons who are favourably disposed. Do not be niggardly, for they are inexhaustible. . . . I will remember those who place their trust in thy prayers. . . . I appoint thee the heiress of my Heart and of all its treasures for time and for eternity, and permit thee to dispose of them according to thine own desires."

" He told me that he would reward an hundred-fold every kindness I received from others."

But it must not be imagined that these revelations diminished the sufferings of St Margaret Mary. On the contrary, they intensified them. For how is it possible for the creature, who is nothing in the sight of God, to attain the power of loving this divine Love as he ought to be loved ? What a perpetual conflict it involves, and how many failures ! The more we strive to become united with God, the more we appreciate his royal condescension. But as our knowledge of God's Love increases, we understand better the infinite distance dividing us from him, and the fundamental impossibility of our poor miserable love ever being able to rise to the height of the infinite. The light shines brighter with every fresh confidence on the part of the Lover, but it is a light that strikes the creature down to earth and overpowers him. Then he cries aloud: " No, Lord, no, thou seest that I cannot rival thy love. It is too great, I am defeated. Withdraw thy favours, for I can do no more."

" He sent three tormenting thoughts into my mind," writes St Margaret Mary, " which were always with me. The first, which was the source of the other two, was a great desire to love him. This was so intense that I imagined that everything which I saw around me should be turned into flames of love whereby he might be loved. Then it was a martyrdom to think how little he is loved. If only I loved him, at least; but I am the most ungrateful of all."

This martyrdom of St Margaret Mary lasted all her life. At the beginning of her life in the convent, she asked Mother Greyfie to teach her how to pray. She was told to go and place herself before the Blessed Sacrament and imagine herself to be a piece of bare canvas.

" No sooner had I begun my prayer, than my Sovereign Master showed me that my soul is this bare canvas on which he desires to depict the details of his life of suffering, his privations, and his sacrifice for love of man. . . . After he had emptied my soul, he inspired me with a great longing to love him and to suffer, so that I could not rest for thinking how I might crucify myself and show my love."

While she was still in the early years of her religious life, she prayed thus:

" I placed myself at his feet as a living victim whose only desire is to be immolated and to be consumed as a burnt-offering in the pure flames of his love."

Her ideal was expressed in these terms:

" We ought to love him so much in this life that we become one with him."

She was tormented by three great desires. " So

overpowering were they that they appeared like three tyrants who subjected me to a perpetual martyrdom without one moment's respite." These three great desires were:

1. To love our Lord with a perfect love.
2. To suffer much for love of him.
3. To die in the transport of this love.

This obsession of love never left her until the near approach of death. Only then was it ousted by the new impulse to acquiesce purely and simply in the will of God. During her last illness she was heard repeating these words:

"Alas, I am burning! What a consolation it would be if it were the love of God that consumed me. But I have never learned how to love my God perfectly."

It is difficult for us to understand this torture of love which feels the martyrdom of its perpetual insufficiency. We have spoken already of her transports of love and fidelity to grace which amounted to a passion. She never refused anything to our Lord: her loving aspirations were continually rising like a burnt-offering to her " Sovereign Lord," or " the Sovereign High Priest," as she called him.

Our Lord asked her "frequently to wound the Heart of her Spouse by ejaculatory prayers, and to keep my heart alert to catch the words he would say to me."

As I have said before, we must not belittle the value of affective love. But without in any way under-estimating the effort of the will as a proof of love—which would be to contradict St Ignatius Loyola and worse still to contradict our Lord himself —we can yet realise the torture of wishing to love without having the power of achievement, or without ever being able to love as we should wish.

" Lord, whatever it may cost," cried St Teresa, " do not permit me any longer to appear before thee empty-handed."[1]

[1] *Life of St Teresa*, by a Carmelite, p. 239.

It is said sometimes that it is easy to love. It is, relatively speaking, easy to act. But can anyone who has tried venture to say that it is easy to love ? There is in love a curious power of suffering. Nothing tortures our poor hearts so much as love. If the words " fever, burning fire " and a hundred others that express suffering are used to describe love among human beings, how can the insatiable longing to be one with God be adequately described ?

When St Gertrude began to feel a desire for a deeper interior life, our Lord came to her—he appeared as a boy of about sixteen years of age— and asked her to hold out her hand and place it in his.

" I was deeply moved, and when I opened my eyes and tried to draw near to thee, I saw between thee and me . . . (from thy right hand to my left) a hedge of such length that neither behind or before me could I discern the end of it. The summit was so thickly covered with thorns, that it was impossible to find any way to reach unto thee, the only consolation of my soul."

The Saint pictures the soul that yearns for God with all its energies and feels the abyss that lies between it and God, between the finite and the infinite. For an instant he has enjoyed a fuller possession of God, and now has the bitter grief of keeping watch over an empty tomb, or rather (since the divine Guest is always there, it is only that his presence is hid from sight) beside a tabernacle where the Divinity is so hidden that only by an act of faith can it realise his presence.

Theodélinde Debouché, the foundress of the *Congregation of Perpetual Adoration*, comparing exterior sacrifices with this interior suffering, gives the palm to the latter. " I have my longings," she says; meaning that these were the chief source of her sufferings.

A few instants of rare possession of the Loved One

are the reward of long moments spent in fruitless
search. "Rara hora, et parva mora!" cried St
Bernard. How the soul longs for the beloved
embrace and the blessed intimacy to be experienced
once more.

"When the Word withdraws himself, the soul
has but one cry that is heard incessantly, one desire
ceaselessly reiterated, one word repeated over and
over again until the Beloved one has returned: 'Come
back, oh, come back!'"

St Bernard, commenting on the words of our
Lord, "a little while and you shall see me,"[1] says:
"This little while, this little while, what a long while
it is! Sweet Saviour, dost thou call it short? A
short time passed without seeing thee. I do not
wish to wrong thee, but thou speakest not in exact
terms. This space of time is terribly long!"[2]

There is perhaps nothing that so clearly expresses
the sufferings of Purgatory as this insatiable thirst
of the loving soul. It has seen God, or rather it has
glimpsed something of the glory of God in the light
which illumined the night of prayer. He who has
once drunk will thirst again. Henceforth he will
have an arrow in his heart, an arrow drawn from
the quiver of St Teresa of Avila.

"Although God has been with me," cried Mary
of the Incarnation, a Canadian Ursuline, "now he
seems to flee from me."

These words are very true. The soul has him,
and then apparently he is gone. And when his
presence is felt, how scant it is! At every moment it
seems as if it would disappear. One longs to embrace
the Loved One; but it is impossible, there is no chance
of succeeding. Can this be called a life, this perpetual torment?

"It is impossible to say what suffering this love
can cause . . . and yet the soul never wishes to be

[1] St John xvi.   [2] *In Cantica*, lxxiv, 2, 3-4.

free of it until it possesses the Beloved. It is as
if it had arms continually outstretched to embrace
him."

The following words, so pregnant with the anguish
of impotent love, are uttered by a writer of our own
days.

" I suffer most of all from my inability to love
Jesus our Victim. . . . I thirst for this love; it is
a devouring thirst which nothing can satisfy; it
causes me a perpetual martyrdom which is the more
painful because the soul has to bear it alone. . . .
This poor soul can do no more, it has reached the end
of its strength. On one side it is overwhelmed by
the love and mercy of Jesus, and on the other it is
crushed to earth by its utter inability to do anything
for him."

The torture of mind is increased by yet another
thought: not only is this Love too mighty, but the
soul is all unworthy of it.

My Jesus, what happiness is thine, for never hast
thou known the terrible grief of having sinned.
Although thou didst fall on the road to Calvary, yet
never like the sinner didst thou fall from grace.
Dost thou realise, O spotless Lamb of God, the
misery of our sinful state, how we feel within us
the inclination to evil. We know that a mere
nothing can kindle afresh the fire of concupiscence
that smoulders in the volcano-like depths of the
soul, ready at any moment to break forth into flame.
Jesus, is our plight known to thee? There is a
well-known story, handed down from ancient times,
which tells of a child who carried a fox in a fold of
his cloak, and of how the animal gnawed his flesh.
In our case the fox is not to be found in a fold of
cloth, but in the uttermost recesses of our being,
and it gnaws at our soul.

But surely the saints cannot experience this
torment, though the sinner may well lament his

unworthiness. The fact is that the nearer the soul is to God, the more clearly it realises its unworthiness. The closer Love approaches, the greater is the sense of the distance between the soul and the Lover. St Margaret Mary dwells upon this. She says that she corresponds but feebly with God's grace; she fears lest she be but " the shadow of a good nun." She knows by experience that there are many luke-warm religious even among the most fervent communities. Had not our Lord asked her one day to make reparation for the negligences committed in her own convent ? Her Sovereign Lord required of her " all or nothing." She knew this well, and again and again she told her novices and her correspondents that the Master did not want a divided heart.

On many occasions she asked herself whether her own negligence was not the chief obstacle to the propagation of the devotion to the Sacred Heart, so greatly desired by her Sovereign Lord. Our Lord had to appease her himself, by clothing her with a white robe.

" See, I have taken away all trace of malice from thy will for evermore, so that for the future thy failings will be a source of humiliation for thee rather than an offence against me. Then once more he opened his adorable Heart, and placing me within it he said: ' Here is thy dwelling-place now and for ever, where thou canst keep unstained the robe of innocence with which I have clothed thy soul.' "

These words may be a difficulty to some, who may say that it is impossible for an act to be a fault and yet not be displeasing to God. It should be remembered, however, that there are certain faults which are only semi-deliberate, or due merely to frailty. While deliberate venial sins are a definite offence against God, these other faults, which are due largely to inadvertence and to the fact that our free will has hardly had time to check the tendency of our lower nature, are permitted by God to humiliate us and make us realise our weakness. " Such faults," says Fr. de Smet, " do not impede our progress in grace. One may almost say ' on the contrary.' "

Although St Margaret Mary was at peace as regards her failings, yet her interior trials did not come to an end.

For her own part she made every effort to be absolutely faithful to her Master, and gave him the affection of her whole heart. But what about the rest of the world ? How many there were who neglected to love the eternal Love ! Especially from the moment of the great revelation, when our Lord said to her: " Behold this heart . . . which receives only scorn and ingratitude," the Saint led a life of continual mortification. Her desire was not so much to make reparation for the wicked by satisfying divine justice, as to make satisfaction for outraged love. " Love is not loved," was St Francis of Assisi's perpetual cry. St Margaret Mary wanted to call out to the whole world that Jesus thirsts to be loved by all mankind. She did all that she could to spread the devotion to the Sacred Heart: if necessary, she would have written to the King. She tried to persuade her superiors to adopt the practice, and in spite of her natural shrinking, she even spoke of it to her directors.

For her novices she designed the first pictures of the Sacred Heart, with an afterthought that these reminders of the love of God himself might go forth to the uttermost ends of the earth and ultimately would induce the world to love him. But after all, what was the use ? How could a poor unknown Visitation nun make known the Sacred Heart of our divine Lord to a cold world ?

Here again is the martyrdom of human impotence. A pious soul, Marguerite Romanet, longed to veil every crucifix. She could not bear to see them.

She could not bear to see Love hanging upon the Cross waiting in vain for someone to love him. " Behold this heart . . . which in return receives only scorn and ingratitude."

In the chapel of the château of Warelle, near Enghien in Belgium, there is an old picture, of no artistic value, which represents our Lord on the cross, with Mary Magdalen kneeling at his feet, her two arms outstretched to prevent the centurion from piercing the side of Jesus. Does not this symbolise the pious ambition of these holy souls ? They would stay the lance and turn it against themselves. They would have God prevent so many unhappy creatures from continuing to crucify our Lord.

CHAPTER III

COMPENSATION BY A LIFE OF SELF-SACRIFICE BEFORE AND AFTER HER TIME

I

IN the preceding chapter we have given a concrete example of a life of reparation in all its details, drawn from the writings of the Saint who, above all others, made it her life-work. Now we way briefly describe in abstract the various elements of which this idea of reparation is composed.

From the foregoing data it may be concluded that the offering of self as a victim of reparation is actuated by a complex motive—complex as the idea of the redemption. It includes God the Father, Jesus Christ, and all mankind.

The almighty power of *God* is outraged by our sins. Homage to his divine Majesty will compensate for the blasphemies or indifference of so many of his creatures. The love of our Lord *Jesus Christ* for mankind is scorned by many souls. To counter-balance so much hatred and mockery great love will be offered to him.

Many *souls* are being carried along to the brink of the abyss and risking eternal loss. A surplus of merit will be gained so that God may touch the hearts of these sinners and not let the blood of Christ be shed for them in vain.

This last aspect of compensation is closely akin to —in fact, includes—the idea of " completion," of which we shall speak later; so true is it that life and vital activity cannot be separated into water-tight compartments.

Of the three aspects of compensation above mentioned each will be emphasised to a greater or smaller degree by individual souls, according to their respective temperaments and the grace that is given them. But in the thoughts of all those who are devoted to a life of reparation these three motives whether singly or simultaneously will always be found. It may be of use to illustrate this by a few examples, some of them belonging to a period antecedent to St Margaret Mary, others of a later date.

One day the eternal Father said to St Mary Magdalen dei Pazzi:

" The wickedness of creatures is so great that were it not that my anger is appeased by my elect and by the spouses of the divine Word, my vengeance would be such that thou wouldst not be able to bear the sight. Do not let thyself slumber in cowardly indifference, but together with my elect, set to work to make expiation for the many outrages that are committed against me and against my truth. Understand that those who remain inactive before sin render themselves thereby in some sort its accomplices. The iniquities of mankind cry aloud for vengeance with greater force even than the blood

of Abel. . . . O my daughter, do not cease to
offer the blood of my Son to me to appease my wrath.
See how all mankind is within the devil's clutch, and
his mouth is open to devour them. Far from
avoiding it, they are throwing themselves into it.
There is not one who will escape unless my elect save
them by their prayers. For my part, I write down
in a book unknown to thee all the iniquities of the
wicked, and beside them, the succour rendered to
them by my elect. . . . At the day of judgement
I shall open this book before the divine Word."[1]

We have here a specifically Christian form of
prayer, the offering of Jesus Christ to the Father.
It is an elementary truth of dogma that our Lord is
the one true " religious," as Olier called him, for he
is the one person who practises the virtue of religion
as required by the infinity of God the Father. He
alone is capable of offering to God the praise that
he deserves, the supplication and the expiation that
are his due.

One day God revealed to St Bridget a glimpse of
the glory of heaven. She heard God ask: " What
does the earth deserve ?" And the angels replied:
" It is worthy of hell-fire." " But," adds St Bridget,
" fortunately the love of our Lord tempered the just
sentence."

It is a striking fact that although in the Old
Testament it is to his just rights that God makes
most frequent appeal, although even in the New
Testament he insists upon them when it is his good
pleasure to do so, nevertheless our divine Master
always prefers to make appeal to our love.

Long before the famous visions of 1689 he appealed
for pious souls who would make some return for his
love: " Thou at least !" is the almost invariable
refrain of the divine Beggar. It is a mystery that
he should prize so highly these miserable love-tokens

[1] *Les Divines Paroles*, Saudreau, i, pp. 187-8.

which he comes to beg from poor human nature. But it is proper to goodness to love even when there is nothing lovable in the object loved.

Fortunately our Lord finds from time to time certain human beings who are a credit to humanity: the Saints. To some of these he has revealed his desires. " Thou hast revealed to me," says St Gertrude, " that being weary of the persecutions and insults that thou receivest from certain souls, thou desirest to come and rest in my heart."

The same has happened in the case of hundreds of privileged souls, women for the greater part. Some people say that women are particularly favoured because they are more affectionate, others say that the reason lies in their more vivid imagination. Even if this last be true of certain hysterical individuals, of whom the Church has shown neither approval nor disapproval, it is false as regards the great authentic saints.

" Frequently," writes Mother Mary of the Divine Heart (Droste-Vischering)," our Lord expressed his desire to take up his abode in my heart as a refuge when the world forgets him, and to enjoy conversing with me as the spouse with his espoused wife."

On April 7, 1898, he repeated the same request: " He told me that he desired to find a human heart which would afford him a place of rest and consolation made ready for him by love and suffering, that he had chosen my heart, without any merit of mine, and that it was to be an altar whereon everything should be consumed in the flames of divine love."

Sister St Peter, the Carmelite of Tours, whose name is familiar to us in the history of the devotion of the Holy Face, tells us that the Master said to her:

" What a grief it is for my heart to see that the grace which cost me so dear should be scorned. Ask of my Father as many souls as the drops of blood which I shed in my Passion. . . . On those loving

hearts who propagate the work of reparation and,
like St Veronica, wipe my adorable face, I will place
the imprint of my features as a reward for their
zeal."

To Gemma Galgani, in Italy, our Lord makes
the same appeal.

" ' What ingratitude and wickedness there is in the
world! Sinners perish in the way of evil. Vile and
lukewarm souls make no effort to conquer their
wicked passions; those who are in sorrow are utterly
overcome and plunged into despair. Every day the
general indifference increases, there is no one who
makes any effort to rouse himself. . . . The thought
of my Sacred Heart and my love never enters their
minds. I am forgotten as if I had never loved them
and suffered for them, as if I were a stranger to them
all.' Jesus would have continued speaking, but I
was obliged to say to him: ' Jesus, Jesus, I cannot bear
any more.' "[1]

In point of fact the Passion is ever being renewed;
Herod, Pilate, the Sanhedrin, the populace are
always with us; each in their turn continues to attack
our Lord.

" O Lord Jesus Christ," cries a convert, Giovanni
Papini, " mankind does thee all the harm that it can;
more so after thy death than during thy life. All
of us are guilty including myself, who speak to thee.
Thousands like Judas have kissed thee after having
sold thee, not once only nor merely for thirty pieces
of silver. Legions of Pharisees and men like Caiaphas
have judged thee to be a malefactor and deserving to
be crucified, and millions of times by their thoughts
they have crucified thee. A vulgar mob strikes thee
on the face, and spits upon thee. Thousands of
Pilates splendidly attired in black and red, fresh
from their toilet, combed, shaved and perfumed,
have delivered thee hundreds of times to the execu-

[1] *Gemma Galgani*, Saudreau, 1903, pp. 126-128.

tioners after having recognised thy innocence.
Innumerable drunken voices have demanded that
the criminal, the seditious, and assassin should be
set at liberty, while thou shouldst be dragged up to
Mount Calvary and there fastened to the wood of
the cross with nails forged by fear and riveted by
hatred. . . ." '

We are so cold and indifferent that we can gaze
unmoved upon this spectacle. Our eyes remain
dry, our hearts do not beat more quickly. The
Passion is one of the facts of history which we have
always known. By this time we are inured to the
thought of it. Those who have the great gift of
prayer know how to be ever " renewing their youth,"
how to give a new meaning to old words, a new
aspect to familiar sights, a new soul to texts that
have been meditated upon a hundred times.

" Frequently our Lord complained of lack of
love on the part of mankind, and my heart was so
deeply wounded by this, that I experienced the
sufferings of hell-fire. . . . I was consumed by this
interior fire: I suffered greatly for the sins of im-
modesty and of scandal. Jesus Christ said to me:
' My children are snatched out of my arms to be
given over to the Evil One and thrown into the
eternal flames.' Then he lovingly asked me:
' Wouldst thou not like to make amends to my Heart
for the scorn and ingratitude of men ?' I replied:
' What can I do, for I am more wretched and ungrateful than they are ?' He said: ' Open thy heart
and thou shalt suffer with me.' Then he caused me
to share in his agony; he showed me how the anger
of the heavenly Father was on the point of breaking
forth to strike all sinners. I offered our Lord and
myself with him. I said: ' Strike me and spare
them one day more.' He told me that he would
grant all that I asked of him. . . . I abandoned

¹ *Storia di Cristo*, by Giovanni Papini, pp. 542, 543.

myself to him as a victim and said: ' Lord, give me
thy love, grant me the salvation of souls, and that
is enough. . . .' I have written down that I will
accept all the crosses that God sees fit to send me;
and after much reflection I have deliberately signed
it.   Further, I have renounced all the merits that I
may gain by my sufferings, leaving them to the
Sacred Heart to dispose as he sees best. . . . I
reserve for myself only his mercy and his love and
give up all the rest. . . .''[1]

Mother Mary of Jesus (of Deluil-Martigny), to
whom fuller reference will be made later, speaks of
having the same reproaches made to her by our Lord,
and of the sufferings of her soul when she received
these terrible revelations from the divine Master.

" I am not known, I am not loved, I am a treasure
that no one appreciates.   I wish to make souls who
will understand me.   I am a torrent that cannot
retain its water, but wants to overflow its banks.
I want souls who will receive these waters.   I want
to make vessels to be filled with the ocean of my
love. . . .   I will do wonders.   Nothing can hinder
me, neither the wiles of Satan nor the unworthiness of
mankind.   I thirst for souls who shall appreciate
me and allow me to fulfil the objects for which I am
here. . . .   I suffer outrage and I am profaned.
Before the end of time I desire to receive reparation
for all the outrages that I have suffered. . . .   I wish
to dispense all the graces that have been refused."

Which is to have the mastery, our own gross self-
love, or the merciful designs of our Saviour Jesus
Christ ?

We have given examples of compensation made
in justice to the Father and out of love for Jesus
Christ.   Here are some acts of reparation offered
out of compassion for mankind.

[1] *Letter* written by the Foundress of the Congregation of
our Saviour and our Lady.

St Catherine of Genoa was present at the exorcism of one who was possessed. When she heard the devil cry out: " I am this miserable being who is deprived of love," the thought of there being on earth men who are the devil's prey and, like him, deprived of love, caused her indescribable grief. . . .

In the heart of every man the fire of charity should be burning, but in how many the flames no longer rise because the fire has gone out ?

" What is thy name ?" " I am the cold," was the Devil's reply to the question of St Bridget; and no description is more true. Her heart is devoured by the longing to enkindle in herself and in others a spark that shall consume the whole earth.

" Lord, let me suffer all the pains thou seest fit; take my joys, my life, but give me souls," was the cry of Mgr. d'Outremont.

" See the spouse who is the Church," said our Lord to St Catherine of Siena, " and note how those who seek the interior life, who seek the fruit of my blood, are lacking." " And I cried: 'What can I do, O my unspeakable Love ?' ' Offer thy life anew and give thyself no rest; it is for this that I have chosen thee and all those who follow thee and will follow thee in the future. . . .' And I exclaimed: 'Eternal God, receive the sacrifice of my life. I have only what thou hast given me. Take my heart and put it under the press, for the sake of thy spouse the Church.' And he took me with such violence that if he had not strengthened me I should have died."

Our Lord appeared with torn garments to St Peter of Alexandria and told him that this robe signified the Church which was rent by the Arian heresy, and reparation had to be made.

How frequently during the course of ages our Lord has repeated this request !

On the feast of the Purification he said to St Margaret of Cortona:

" Know that the world will suffer various afflictions for the sins it has committed. The multitude of men's iniquities has increased so greatly during this century that, I confess, I hardly dare to pray to my Father foɪ them. Even my mother, the advocate of sinners, fears to plead to me her Son for them, because of their many iniquities."

In point of fact, great calamities at that time fell upon England, France, Rome, Tuscany, and Sicily. Who shall say if they had not some relation with the sins of which our Lord spoke ?

On the Second Sunday of Advent he said to her:

" I warn thee that sinners will have to suffer bitter tribulations, for before the close of this century, the scourge of plague, fire and war will come upon them. The stench of their evildoing, both of body and soul, has risen up before me and I will bear it no longer. The malice of Christians at this present time in the invention of fresh crimes surpasses that of the Jews in my Passion."

The efforts made by the Saint after these revelations to obtain mercy may be imagined. God is always the same God. In the Old Testament we read how the anger of God was appeased by the prayer of Moses, and now also he works in the same manner. It is fortunate that it is so; it is well that mercy and justice should kiss. Our Lord requires a greater measure of love and acts of reparation from the more generous souls. " He showed me the number of people who fall into hell," writes Sister Saint Peter, the Carmelite of Tours, " and in the most touching way asked me to help these poor sinners. He made known to me the strict obligation under which Christian people are to assist these unhappy blind creatures; for if intercession is made for them, he, of his mercy, will open their eyes."

There were three sisters who all made a freewill offering of themselves to suffer for " the salvation of sinners." One of them, Caroline, said to her spiritual father:

" I thirst to suffer; I must tell you the reason why. It is for the sake of sinners. . . . The desire for the salvation of souls torments me more and more; at moments I repeat more than fifty times the words: ' God, have mercy upon sinners.' "

Another time she wrote—and it is difficult to say whether her compassion for our Lord or her pity for sinners is more to be admired:

" For many long years past my most urgent desire has been to make reparation and obtain the mercy of God for myself and for others. To see how God is offended causes me acute pain. That is why my whole mind and heart are set upon suffering and pains of all sorts, and why I am always asking for them. I welcome them into my heart, and open it wide so that it may suffer all the torture and anguish that it is capable of enduring with the aid of divine grace. I make an offering not only of my heart, but of my whole self and of all the powers of my mind. And in the constant renewal of these pains my acute sorrow finds relief, because thereby I hope to be able to make amends in a small way to the good God for all that he suffers from my sins and the flood of iniquities on earth.

" Jesus alone knows the martyrdom which I have been enduring for years: he sees the tears I have shed because I have seen him so greatly offended. He knows that I do not exaggerate when I say that I suffer a thousand agonies and a thousand deaths at the sight of the crimes that are constantly committed against him. His love and grace are scorned and trodden under foot."

II

Acts of reparation are required for all kinds of iniquities, for blasphemy, impurity, and indifference, for confessions hurried by routine or openly bad, for sacrilegious Communions, for the neglect of Communion. Then there are acts of compensation to be made—and these are not the least in importance, as we have seen in speaking of St Margaret Mary—for his " chosen people."

A few examples will suffice here:

On December 28, 1856, Mother Veronica of Jesus, known in the world as Mary Caroline Lioger, the foundress of the *Congregation des Sœurs Victimes du Cœur de Jesus*, had a striking vision of the evils that afflict the Church. She tells us:

" I saw a chalice appearing in the sky, and over it the Sacred Host and the cross. I immediately fell on my knees; the Host was being assailed by a thousand darts from all sides. They touched it, but without overthrowing it, and the fury of the attackers was at its height. It was then that I saw a real persecution going on in the sky, and I heard a voice say: ' These attack me in the practice of their religion.' The anger of God seemed to be aroused by acts of profanation, sacrileges, unworthy communions. And all the while, as was my custom, I cried: ' Mercy, Lord. . . .' Then our Lord said to me: ' My one desire is to pardon, but come thou and assist at the judgement of the nations.' I saw what I should never have believed to be true, that in the body of the Church itself the number of the just was so small that I was petrified with horror."

No mention is made here of the sins of the wicked. It would be superfluous to speak of them, for the wicked will not read this book. But there are the sins of the good, which cause much greater suffering to the Sacred Heart, the offences of " those who call themselves his friends," which can be found, alas! among the priesthood and in the cloister.

St Catherine of Ricci, while she was addressing an exhortation to her daughters on October 13, 1553, fell into an ecstasy, and repeated to them the words which our Lord had told her to say to them:

" Their cross consists in the observance of the three vows, the rule and the constitutions, yet few of them trouble about it, or if they do think of it, it is the last thought which comes to their minds, instead of being, as it should, the first and most important. . . . What more can I do for thee and for them ? The graces which are lacking to them are those of which they have voluntarily deprived themselves either by their bad dispositions or because they did not ask for them, nor seek nor want them. I only waited to give them until I saw they were earnestly desired and asked for. Precious gems and pearls are not given to those who do not appreciate their value; neither do I accord my gifts and favours to those who do not prize them. . . . They no longer remember me, they have almost forgotten to love me. Yet are they not consecrated to my service, to be zealous for my glory ? Do they not see what is going on in the world, and how few there are who think of me ? . . . I am far from desiring them to be depressed beyond measure, to lose courage, or to be overcome by my reproaches. I only wish to see them confidently returning to me. Let them come unto me; I am waiting for them with arms outstretched upon the cross."[1]

Our Lord explained to St Veronica Giuliani that there were three things which caused him great displeasure " in monasteries and convents."

1. Lack of respect towards the Superior.
2. Want of charity and sharp tongues.

[1] *Vie*, by P. H. Bayonne.

3. The habit of living too comfortably, and not according to holy poverty.

Why is it, alas! that the same complaints made periodically are powerless to overcome this unvarying lukewarmness and inertia? Let it not be said of us that we permit these sorrowful appeals to pass unheeded.

For sins of cowardice and sensuality our Lord demands multiform acts of reparation. Self-immolation there must always be, for suffering has to restore the balance lost by the pleasure of sinning; but it can be expressed in many different ways. Sometimes it will take the form of bodily penance, and of the most austere type.

Mary Brotel was asked by our Lord to make her bed on the floor in reparation for the sins committed at night.

Blessed Mary d'Oignies witnessed a horrible action which made such an impression upon her innate purity that she took off her shoe and made a cut with a knife on the sole of her foot, then with her bleeding foot she walked up and down, offering the pain she was suffering and the shedding of her blood to make amends for the outrage committed against God, and to efface the stain of that sin. And let those who might be shocked at such an action remember that in the life of St Margaret Mary and of many others we find traces of mortifications from which our minds, which in this matter are perhaps somewhat pharisaical, are inclined to shrink in horror.

" Our Lord made known to me," writes Mother Mary of the Divine Heart, " that when the mystical body of the Church requires help in some way, he often sends bodily sufferings, illnesses, etc., to one of his spouses in order to obtain the necessary graces."

There are certain people for whom this sacrifice

of their lives would be a risky proceeding. Here, more than elsewhere, there must be prudence and obedience to authority. Many fervent souls, even, are lacking in good sense and are ill-balanced. Piety will always be meritorious, but it may be a great danger—especially for the spiritual director—if it is not combined with prudence.

Peter Lafon, when he was a scholar at the seminary of Notre Dame-des-Champs, was taken with his comrades one day in Holy Week, as usual, to venerate the relics of the Passion at Notre Dame in Paris. In that year (1894) a ciborium had been stolen. When Peter Lafon heard of the sacrilege which had been committed that very morning, he offered himself on the spot as a victim of expiation to repair the crime.

Would God accept this act of youthful generosity? The following week the boy fell ill and went to bed; the doctor was reassuring and said it was only a light attack of scarlatina. But the child knew he would not recover. " Mamma," he said, " it is God's will." Soon afterwards, his arms held up in the form of a cross by two of his sisters, he died.

But more often it is by mental sufferings that reparation is made for evildoing. The act of consent to sin takes place in the will, in the centre of our being. And it is there, within us, that the altar of sacrifice should be prepared, and the victim offered. There is interior desolation, an insatiable torturing thirst which is always longing for the salvation of the world, and numberless forms of interior purgation. From time to time our Lord reveals some of the torments suffered by the lost, to some soul that is more especially filled with the desire to make reparation. There is no form of suffering to equal this pain.

If God spares the chosen victim, the victim will not be sparing of himself.

Perhaps—and this is more frequently the case—
he will not be asked to shed his blood, but rather
to give up his will. He will exert himself to be
perfectly responsive to grace. This is true martyrdom; there is less danger of rashness, and it costs
greater effort. Sometimes the desire to be faithful
in all things takes the form of a vow—the vow of
servitude, or of perfection, or of immolation. We
have seen examples of this, and we need not develop
the theme.

Are there many who embrace a life of voluntary
self-immolation ? God alone knows. Some com-
plain that devoted souls who lead a life of true self-
sacrifice are becoming rarer. The writer may be
wrong; but as far as he can judge, the contrary is the
truth.

PART III

COMPLETION

CHAPTER I

OUR SHARE IN THE WORK OF REDEMPTION
BETTER UNDERSTOOD

I

WE are all familiar with those mysterious words of St Paul: " I fill up those things that are wanting of the sufferings of Christ, in my flesh, for his body, which is the Church."[1]   There is no need to dwell upon the doctrinal aspect of the text, but in conformity with the plan underlying this volume, we have to establish the fact.   After St Paul and the many early fathers who so frequently refer to the mystical body of Christ and our power of making reparation, it seems (I say " it seems " advisedly, to leave room for correction if I am wrong) that the doctrine of our obligatory co-operation with the sacrifice of Christ, which follows from our intimate union with his person, became somewhat obscured and neglected by the majority of the faithful.   Many, indeed, derived great spiritual benefit from it, but it was less openly and explicitly professed.   It was like those streams which at a certain point vanish underground and later on reappear above the ground. Their water rendered more limpidly clear by passage through the earth, their volume swelled by the influx of other springs.

Similarly this pregnant theology of St Paul which

[1] Col. i 24.

95

teaches that the Christian is not only one of the
redeemed, but also a redeemer of his brethren,
although familiar to the early ages, was neglected
for some time.   At length, in the nineteenth century,
it emerged once more to the surface and began again
to set its impress more clearly upon the piety of the
faithful.

In the Middle Ages, as we have seen, the mind
dwelt upon the wounds of our Lord. Men did not
reason, they gazed upon them and that was sufficient.
Christ had suffered. They wanted to suffer too.
As little St Elizabeth of Hungary imitated her
mother's actions in church, so they desired to
impress the acts of Christ crucified upon their daily
lives. Theirs was contemplation in the Ignatian
sense of the word, rather than a meditation wherein
all the powers of the soul are used. The mind is
fixed upon the cross; it does not think about the
theology of the cross.

Later on contemplation partakes more of the
character of meditation: there is more reasoning.
No longer is the Cross isolated from everything else;
it is set in its proper perspective as the pivot of
the world's history, and the ingratitude of the world
is more fully realised.

On Calvary our Lord is not contemplated alone.
The soldiers are there who forced the crown of thorns
upon his head; the executioners who drove in the
nails; the centurion who pierced his side.   And the
longing to imitate our Lord becomes, above all, a
wish to protect him.

It is more exact, perhaps, to say that it is less the
thought of the cross than that of the agony in the
garden which attracts men's minds.   Their thought
constantly comes back to the interior sufferings of
him who was wounded for our transgressions.

At the present time the "meditation" element
is becoming more common. Men think about the

philosophical, or rather the theological, aspect of the Redemption.   And if a choice has to be made between the crucifixion, the agony in the garden, and the sacrifice of the Mass, it is perhaps this last which rivets the attention more closely.   Here there is less to catch the eye.   The sacrifice is purely mystical; there is no shedding of blood, and the appeal to the senses is reduced to the minimum.   Reflection alone comes into play.

Meditation upon our Lord and the thought of the long delay in the coming of his kingdom induces us to offer ourselves for this object.   We think of him and love him less as our Saviour than as the Lord who has laboured in vain, whose work, in respect of so many souls, has been fruitless.   We want to help those who are perishing so that the precious Blood may not have been shed in vain.

In vain !   The word fills us with horror.   Why is it that after 1900 years such sufferings of mind and body have produced so small a result?   Does it not seem as if Calvary were in part a failure ?   And we ask ourselves if perhaps we are not responsible for this failure.   We have forgotten who Christ is, and what is the meaning of the fulness of Christ. We have too readily lost sight of the truth that we are one with Christ, and that therefore every Christian soul should take part in the redemption of the world.

Not that we must forget to suffer with Christ. There has appeared lately a life of Christ which is destined to reach a wider public than is usually the case with religious books.   In the closing paragraph it voices the plaintive cry of the Christian soul: " We, the latter-day Christians, await thee.   Every day we look for thee although all unworthy and almost despairing.   All the love that remains in these hearts, which human passions have exhausted, will be thine, O Crucified One, who didst suffer

7

torments for love of us, and now tormentest us with
the strength of thy insatiable love !"[1]

These are not mere empty words. In our day, as
in earlier times, both in the cloister and in the world,
there are individuals longing to sacrifice themselves
out of pity for the sorrows of Christ crucified. The
desire to make amends is also very widespread. In the
following quotation the desire to sympathise and
the longing to make amends are closely intermingled:

" I cannot any longer resist the appeals of divine
grace, and in spite of the rebellion of nature and the
distaste which is ever rising up anew, when I realise the
anguish my Jesus endured for love of me, and the salvation of souls, grace gains the victory. Since he asks
me to share his bitter sufferings, I will not leave him
to bear them alone, more especially when I see so
many who abandon him. A single soul costs very
dear, and much suffering is required in order that the
fruits of our Lord's Passion may be applied to it. . . ."[2]

The following extract is taken from the notes
of Miss Tamisier, the enthusiastic and persevering
pioneer of international Eucharistic processions.

" Processions of the Blessed Sacrament have been
sacrilegiously suppressed in many parts of the land.
Therefore crowds of people from all quarters of
France should flock to Lourdes in reparation, with
banners representing the different towns and villages.
How splendid it would be if the men would form an
escort for the Blessed Sacrament, and walk with
bare feet, thinking upon their own sins and the sins
of their country. It would be finer still if they would
gather round the crowned statue of our Lady and,
lifting up their right hands, in a loud voice renew
their baptismal promises, and dedicate themselves to
our Lord for ever."

[1] *Storia di Cristo* (Italian edition), by Giovanni Papini,
p. 549.
[2] *Caroline Clement*, by Father Henry, C.SS.R., p. 582.

II

There are many, and the number is daily increasing, whose preference lies rather in seeking to diminish the sufferings of our Lord than in grieving over them and offering their sympathy. They wish to take them upon themselves, to regard them as their own.

General de Sonis writes:

" Blessed be thou, my God, when thou triest me. I desire to be broken, consumed and utterly destroyed by thee, to be more and more annihilated. I do not seek to be one of the polished carven stones of the building, but a paltry grain of sand that has been taken from the dust of the road. May I be crucified, Jesus, but crucified with thee !"

Our generous actions cannot actually take away any of the sufferings of our divine Master. From the morning of Easter, our glorified risen Saviour can no longer undergo the smallest suffering. So he cannot at the present time be spared actual pain. But he may, and does, know now that he was relieved of suffering in the past, and it is the joy of being able to afford this relief which took place long ago that is the incentive to acts of renunciation at the present day. The fact that a cause had its effect in the past does not prevent it from being an actual cause. It depends upon us now whether Christ suffered more or less at the time of his agony and death upon the cross.

There is another way also of showing the wonderful actuality of our daily acts of generosity. Sins, my sins and the sins of others, are the cause of Christ's Passion. Therefore if the number of sins is lessened, the sufferings of Christ are diminished. And then we think of the fate of souls. Souls are actually now being saved, actually now being lost.

If I can succeed in causing the blood of Christ to

be less unfruitful, I shall relieve the great pain of the Sacred Heart. Are we not filled with sorrow when we gaze upon the crucifix, and penetrating beyond the actual representation, the ivory figure upon a mother-of-pearl or ebony cross, see the real Crucified Saviour of flesh and blood nailed to the rough wood? We strive to imagine what were the last thoughts of our Saviour in his death agony. Across the span of centuries we seem to see the heart-breaking look of those eyes in his last moment when he seems to be saying to himself: "Nineteen hundred years hence where will be the world, and what will be the fruits of my Passion? Out of fifteen hundred million human beings, there will be a thousand million heathen. Out of the five hundred millions who will know my name, half will have lapsed into heresy or schism, and only the other half will be Catholic and able therefore to share fully in my sacrifice. Moreover, of these two hundred and seventy-two million Catholics, how many can be numbered among the faithful? Nothing is lacking to my sacrifice, yet what return is this, to be so ill-treated by man, I, the Son of God, who have come amongst them? How many there are throughout the ages who will not benefit by my sacrifice!"

It is true that man can be saved without belonging visibly to Christ. Who therefore shall count the transfiguring actions of divine grace and the secret desires of these twelve hundred million souls that are separated from him? Yet what a multitude of souls, and what poor results! There is good reason for pitying our Lord.

Whence comes this failure? How comes it that the precious Blood is relatively, yet none the less flagrantly, of no avail? The slightest gesture of our Saviour was sufficient to redeem the world. Why has his great sacrifice not yielded greater results?

The failure is not on his side, it is on ours. It

must not be forgotten that Christ is not complete alone. He is not his full self—we do not mean in the fulness of his physical body as child of the Father and son of our blessed Lady, but in the integrity of his mystical body—he is not complete unless we his members agree to collaborate with him. By our share in the same Holy Spirit we are united to his Person, and are therefore at the same time and for the same reason closely associated with his work. His work is the Redemption. We cannot, therefore, refuse the office of " redeemers." Further, Christ's work is the redemption of the world by sacrifice. We cannot, therefore, escape the vocation to a life of self-sacrifice.

Christian self-sacrifice now becomes not merely a question of prudence—because our rebellious senses require to be kept in check by mortification—not only a question of justice—because if I have sinned I must make reparation—but also a question of love, and not only of love for Christ, but of love for souls The French school of the seventeenth century, Bérulle, Condren, Olier, although it expressed itself in a somewhat rugged manner, yet with a rare doctrinal knowledge showed the wonderful lessons that can be drawn from the right understanding of the truth of our incorporation with our Saviour Jesus Christ.

Blessed Grignon de Montfort in the eighteenth century, the great apostle of the Breton Calvaries, popularises these great ideas. His *Lettre circulaire aux amis de la Croix*, which was written at the close of one of his retreats, is like a rushing stream of molten lava in its effect. He would have liked to have sealed it with his blood.

He first calls to mind the underlying principle of our union with Christ.

" A friend of the Cross is one whom Christ cruci-fied has illustriously conquered . . . and since he is

born of the Passion, the cross is the very breath of
his life.　He dies to the world, to the flesh, and to sin,
so as to be hidden on earth with Jesus Christ in God.
A friend of the Cross is truly one who carries our
Lord; he is one with Jesus Christ so that in truth it
can be said: " And I live, now not I: but Christ
liveth in me."[1]

Then what should be our conduct ?

" You are members of Jesus Christ: what an
honour !　But the honour carries with it the duty
of suffering.　The head is crowned with thorns, and
his members wear wreaths of roses !　The head is
mocked and besmirched with the mud of the road
to Calvary, and his members are sitting upon thrones
amid sweet perfumes !　The head has no pillow,
while his members sleep delicately on feather beds !
This were an unheard-of monstrosity.　But do not
be deceived; these Christians whom you see on all
sides, fashionably dressed, fastidious in their habits
and manners, are not the true disciples, nor the
real members of Christ crucified.　It would be
insulting to this thorn-crowned Head and contrary
to the gospel-teaching to believe it.　What poor
imitations are these who think themselves to be the
members of our Lord !　They are his most traitorous
persecutors, for while with their hands they make
the sign of the cross, in their hearts they are enemies
of the cross.　If your life is similar to the life of our
Lord upon earth, if you are led by the same spirit,
then you must expect the thorns and nails, and the
scourge—in one word, the cross.　Your Master is
crowned with thorns and the disciple must receive
the same treatment as his Lord, the member as the
head. . . .　You know that you are the living
temples of the Holy Spirit, and as living stones are
destined by the God of love to build up the walls
of the heavenly Jerusalem.　Expect, therefore, to be

[1] Gal. ii 20.

cut, hewn, and chiselled by the hammer of the
cross, or else you will remain like rough blocks
which are useless and contemptuously thrown away.
Be careful not to resist the blows of the hammer,
and be attentive to the hand which wields the
cutting blade. Maybe this loving and accomplished
Architect wishes to make you one of the principal
stones of the eternal city."

The author of *L'Apostolat de la Souffrance*, Father
Lyonnard, S.J., who lived at the close of the last
century, was an active apostle of this great doctrine.
His biography at the beginning of the volume shows
how heroically he led a life of reparation for the
salvation of souls.

He states the principle of the deification of the
Christian, and therefore of Christian suffering. He
fully explains the text of St Paul, " I fill up those
things that are wanting of the sufferings of Christ,"
and then shows how efficaciously we can make
reparation by our sufferings, and also enumerates
the various types of souls who are called to the
practice of this splendid form of apostolate.

From these examples it is clear that a new aspect
of the doctrine—if we may call it new—is especially
emphasised in this period. When it was a case of
offering sympathy and making amends, then the
sinner was regarded chiefly as one who should be
reproved and reproached for his sins, and for whom
loving acts must be made to satisfy the yearnings
of the love of Christ. Now, no longer does wrath fall
upon the sinner; it is realised that he must be saved,
and that our Lord alone is not sufficient. Christ
vouchsafes to be insufficient so as to make use of us.
It is for us to bring him the assistance of our humble
self-sacrifice, the *complement* of our collaboration.

I desire to do this: Christ chooses to act as if he
were not all-powerful. Therefore the Cyrenean and
St Veronica must come to his aid.

It is my duty: without my intervention souls will be deprived of the measure of redemptive grace which would have assured their sanctification or their final salvation.

Thus I do not think only of our Lord in his sufferings, nor merely of his outrages, but I consider him as one who is rendered useless.

The word "useless" is employed relatively, for it is of his own free will that he condescends to call me to work with him.

There is something "wanting," as St Paul says, and I have to fill it up. There is an element lacking in the Passion. We have generously to supply this lack by taking part in the work of redemption. We must *sympathise*, we must *make amends*, and thirdly, we must *complete*.

CHAPTER II

CAUSES OF THIS BETTER UNDERSTANDING

IN these considerations upon the need of completing what is wanting to Jesus Christ in the work of the redemption, it will be interesting to try and discover the various causes that have led to the fuller understanding of this doctrine.

One of these causes is the development of the *social sense*, that is to say, the ever-increasing tendency, at any rate among good people, to regard things from a broader standpoint. The individual is less inclined to isolate himself selfishly in his daily life and religious practices. From the Catholic point of view this means a deeper understanding of the dogma of the Communion of Saints. Other causes are the wonderful expansion of the devotion to the *Sacred Heart* and of love for the *Holy Eucharist*; the greater interest shown in the *Liturgy* of the

Church, and a more widespread attraction *to prayer*, due, largely, to the use of *retreats*.

I

It cannot be denied that the development of the social sense is one of the marked characteristics of the present time.   The best among modern minds, wearied of the individualistic spirit of the Revolution,[1] are trying to obtain a better understanding of our mutual responsibilities.

The notion of solidarity, in spite of its misrepresentations at the hands of its disciples, is becoming popular and more general.   Man regards himself less as an isolated being than as a part of the human race. Even in cases where the belief in eternal happiness has been lost, and with it the hope of a life to come, there remains, at any rate, the desire to ameliorate the condition of the men and women of the future. With this end in view the present generation is called upon to make the necessary sacrifices.

But it is principally the idea of our supernatural solidarity which is gaining ground.   No generation has better understood the meaning of the Communion of Saints.

The following stanzas are taken from the poem entitled *Le Miracle de la Douleur*, by Jean Lionnet:

> Not thou the dried and sterile tree, the corn
> Unharvested, the workmen all unversed:
> No better worker in my vine there is
> Than this poor sufferer resigned, who prays.
> I take his pains that they may bear their fruit,
> Like a refreshing stream their unction shed
> Upon the sinner's feeling of remorse,
> On those who weary of the narrow way;
> And through the years this flood has ever swelled,
> Fed by his agonies, his tears, his prayers,
> His love has warmed the ice-bound earth anew.

---

[1] *Translator's Note.*—In England, the Reformation, and at a later date the teachings of the Manchester school.

The invalid of whom Jean Lionnet is speaking was Huysmans, the historian of St Lydwine, who died of cancer, offering his sufferings to God for the salvation of souls.

It is significant that on the tomb of the poet a layman declared: "The Communion of Saints is not a mere figurative expression, it is a reality. We know full well that the Catholic revival is not due to our own puny efforts, but to the virtues of our dead, to the simple yet none the less wonderful self-sacrifice of the body which lies here."

The well-known writer, Georges Goyau, in his book *Autour du catholicisme social*, frequently refers to the "phenomenon of the communion of saints" and "the social aspect of Catholicism," and has headed two of his chapters with these titles. The same idea occurs in certain passages of Louis Veuillot's *Ça et là*, in a fragment from an address of Albert de Mun on the apostolate of prayer by suffering, and, what is more unexpected, in a commentary on the hymn for the dedication of a church which is to be found in the *Grande pitie des Églises de France*, written by Maurice Barrès.

There are other writers whose aim is to show the capacity for good which the Christian has at his disposal, once he realises his responsibilities in relation to the salvation of the human race.

Emil Baumann puts in the mouth of one of his characters the following eloquent prayer: "May the bleeding of my heart be mingled with the out-pouring of thy precious Blood, and fall drop by drop upon the dead who are suffering."

Another writer, who calls himself the Pilgrim of the Absolute, expresses himself in the following forcible terms:

"Anyone who has not the faith cannot realise the value of a soul, because he does not know what it costs. "You are bought with a great price," says

St Paul.[1] " I know well that you desire the good of your fellow-man, and are ready even to sacrifice yourself for him, but what do you mean by this good ? You speak of improving the lot of those who suffer. But how can you imagine this to be possible when you are only concerned with their material well-being ? and it is impossible for it to be otherwise, since you have nothing to offer their souls. No one has done them so much good as the men of great faith, whom the Church calls the saints. But the saints knew that the human body is only the outward appearance of man, so their labours were directed principally towards the soul, that never dies. They knew also that suffering is supernaturally good for everyone, and that the man who does not suffer, or who is unwilling to suffer, is a disinherited son of the God who was the Man of Sorrows, that only he who accepts pain and sorrow can appreciate the value of his own soul." And in order to impress this idea upon the minds of his readers at all costs, he adds: " You will not maintain as some men do, that neither poverty nor suffering should exist. Who, then, will pay the debt mankind has incurred ?"

Jeanne Galzy, a teacher, describes in her book, *Les Allongés,* the sufferings of those invalids whose limbs have to be placed in a plaster case, as she herself witnessed at Berck. She gives the impressions experienced by one who is capable of recording her thoughts during the time that she is lying immovable upon the plank stretched across the little wheeled chair in which these unfortunate people are carried about. Although she seems to be sympathetic towards Christianity, there is nothing to show that she is a believer; but she finally grasps the power of suffering to make amends, and refuses to believe that so much pain can be of no use.

" Each drop from a festering wound pays some

[1] I Cor. vi 20.

debt. It is the price paid for those who enjoy such superb health and do great things for the future human race. We pay the ransom of the happiness of others. We lie here motionless, while others march onwards. Aided by us humanity is able to continue on its way; we are the counterweight that enables the scale to rise on the other side."

Louis Peyrot, the founder of the *Union catholique des Malades*, expresses the same idea; he glories in the vocation of those chosen souls "who suffer for others. God has taken them with him to bear his Cross, which is for the good of all men. These persons ' fill up,' as St Paul says, ' what is wanting to the Passion of Christ.' Here they are" (he was speaking of the sanatorium at Leysin in Switzerland) "as on another Calvary, suffering for the relief of France and the whole world. I know some who have to bear constant fever, insomnia, wounds, who are obliged to undergo operations because of their physical condition. Some are young and innocent."[1]

On the eve of the Great War in 1914, he wrote:
" In reality the success of the apostolic labours of missionaries, priests, preachers, men and women who work for others, is due even more than we imagine to the hidden merits of some poor unknown sufferer. The passing of the merits of one person to another is a wonderful thing. This expression of the communion of saints is one of the most striking truths of the Christian religion."

Jacques Rivière,[2] writing from the prison of Koenigsbrück, where he was converted in 1916, asks himself: " What shall I do to keep always before me the thought of the sufferings of others ?"

Secular writers have received sufficient attention;

[1] *L'Apostolat d'au Malade*, by Louis Peyrot, pp. 90, 101.
[2] Afterwards editor of the *Nouvelle Revue Française*.

it is time to listen to what priests have to say on this subject.

The Abbé Perreyve reminds us of the words of St Paul: " For as the body is one and hath many members; and all the members of the body, whereas they are many, yet are one body: so also is Christ."[1] He suggests to those who suffer that they should realise that they are parts of one whole, and that they can exercise a most decisive influence upon the rest of the mystical body. For them, as for Christ, the best method of exerting this influence is by suffering. The world can be saved more easily by being nailed to the cross, than by setting off on some long and difficult expedition. Everything depends upon the intensity of love.

" When the children of God are tried by fire, nothing should be further from their thoughts than that they are alone. It may be said, speaking generally, that the word isolation is unchristian; but when it refers to a case of suffering and self-immolation, it is still more untrue. Be careful never to think that your pains are of no account, that the silent conflict, borne in loving patience, can remain barren. Your sufferings are the common treasure of all mankind (united with Christ). And on the day when all things are revealed, you will meet this or that unknown brother whose conversion and subsequent beatitude you have purchased."

Monsignor Benson, confronted by Protestants who deny both the Communion of Saints and the doctrine of merit, states the all-powerful action of suffering in reparation in a fine page of his book, *Christ in the Church*.

" Amongst Catholics alone, again, does it seem to be recognised that the sufferings of the individual benefit the world as a whole—that is to say, that the pain principle of nature is a principle of grace. If

[1] 1 Cor. xii 12.

the Carthusian went into his cloister *merely* in order
to save his soul, there would be something in the
sneer of ' selfishness ' with which he is always
assailed.   For non-Catholics as a rule (and quite
naturally) seem to be unable to regard themselves
as anything but detached units, each wholly self-
contained and self-seeking.   They are entirely without any glimpse of the vision of the Body of Christ,
that vast supernatural organism in which the Lamb
of God mystically suffers always—that organism
in which the agony of one member draws off the
poison from the rest—that organism of which the
most honourable members are those in which Gethsemane manifests itself continually.   This principle
runs through the whole of the Catholic Church from
head to foot.   In her not only is the exterior sacrifice
of the Cross offered without ceasing in the august
mystery of the altar (since what Christ did once he
always does) in one mode; and in another, in the
exterior sufferings of her members; but the interior
pains of Gethsemane are similarly perpetuated."[1]

Monsignor Gay, commenting upon the book
L'Apostolat de la Souffrance, by Père Lyonnard, S.J.,
which at that time had just been published, writes:

" The Church lives by two forms of sacrifice, the
personal sacrifice of Jesus Christ, and the perpetua-
tion of his sacrifice in his members.   Neither the
Mass nor martyrdom can cease while the world lasts.
The sufferings of mind and body, says Père Lyonnard,
are a form of martyrdom, a species of blood-shedding.
This mysterious blood, which escapes through the
wounds made in the Christian heart, partakes of the
atoning virtue of the precious Blood with which
it is united.   Dear souls who suffer, look first at
Jesus Christ: it is your right and your duty so to do,
and there you will obtain strength.   But also with
simple faith and unshaken confidence say to your-

[1] *Christ in the Church*, part iii, pp. 116-117.

selves that in union with our Lord you, on your part, are bearing the burden of the whole world, to save and redeem it. Say to yourselves, crucified souls, that Jesus is the priest in the sacrifice which he offers as he is also the victim, and by the fact of your sufferings, you not only participate in the fruits of this divine sacrifice, but share in the act which constitutes it. You become the hosts of this High Priest, to be offered to God with Jesus and in Jesus, one and the same burnt-offering."

Father Lintelo became in Belgium the apostle of the Holy Eucharist and of the idea of reparation: his zeal equalled that of Father Lyonnard. The offering of his life which he made on his deathbed showed an appreciation of the virtue of self-sacrifice of a very high order. In his biography you may read how he dedicated himself to a life of immolation, and of the various sacrifices with which his generosity inspired him, notably that which he learned from a Jesuit father of distinguished virtue whom he had known at the college of Ghent:

" Jesus, grant me a life that is rough and laborious, crucified and apostolic. Vouchsafe to increase in my soul that hunger and thirst for sacrifice, suffering, and humiliations and self-abasement. Henceforward I desire neither satisfaction nor repose, consolation nor joy. My sole ambition, which I implore thy Sacred Heart to grant me, is to be always and ever increasingly a victim, host, apostle, virgin, and martyr for love of thee."

Many souls under the guidance of Father Lintelo climbed this lofty ascent, and though perhaps they did not reach such heights as he did, yet they found in their devotion to the Holy Eucharist the inspiration for their acts of loving self-immolation.

II

No man or men, however brilliant, even the holiest among them, will have any success in their apostolate of suffering unless their words find some response in the hearts of the Christian people. As a matter of fact, three events have prepared the minds of Christians for a better understanding of the part that they are to play in the redemption. They are: (1) the habit of frequent Holy Communion; (2) a greater devotion to the Sacred Heart; and (3) a better understanding and a keener appreciation of the liturgy and of mental prayer.

The law of action and reaction is of universal application. The better understanding of the dogma of the Communion of Saints and of the apostolic value of self-sacrifice produced a wave of zeal for the spirit of sacrifice. In its turn this wave of zeal for sacrifice was the occasion of a more ample development of the doctrinal grounds upon which it is based, grounds of which many of the most zealous were quite ignorant.

Increased devotion to the Holy Eucharist, more than anything else, has helped in these days to make the faithful understand their obligation to take part in the redemption of the world. Holy Communion especially is a sharing in the *life* of Christ; it is equally a participation in the death of our divine Saviour and therefore in his redeeming sacrifice.

It is at the foot of the Tabernacle that many faithful souls have been inspired with the wish to offer themselves as victims. They see that the Mass is offered by Christ, by the Priest, and by each one of us. Therefore Holy Communion can only have its full significance in the union of the two who are sacrificed, Jesus and the communicant, in the one victim.

In the nineteenth century there was, perhaps, no

one who understood more fully this great truth, or at any rate explained its meaning more clearly, than the generous-hearted foundress of the *Filles du Cœur de Jésus*, Marie Deluil-Martigny.

She was the daughter of a lawyer, and was born on May 28, 1841. It was the superior of the Jesuit house at Marseilles, Father Calage, who encouraged her to follow her attraction towards our Lord as victim.

The guiding principle of her spiritual life is expressed in the following sentence: " The Father's glory is to receive the unending oblation of his Son, and therein that of all mankind. These, saved and regenerated, become once more his children, and, united to the sacrifice of Jesus, are transformed and fused into his oblation."

Her one occupation during prayer was " to offer Jesus and his Precious Blood without ceasing for priests and all those who are consecrated to God, and to offer myself with him."

These last words show the reality of her self-sacrifice; in all things and on all occasions there was the most generous gift of self.

On August 15, 1873, she described her aims as follows:

" Continual union with the sacrifice of the altar, the uninterrupted offering of my heart in union with the chalice which is elevated by the hands of the priest. The constant thought of the sufferings of our crucified Saviour, and especially of the martyr-dom of his adorable Heart. Constant sacrifice in order to be a victim in union with Jesus Christ."

Every day she explained to her daughters how they could fill up what was wanting to the Passion of Christ, and how at the offertory in the Mass they should always place themselves in the chalice of our redemption.

" We will keep ourselves hidden in this divine

chalice like the drops of water that the priest mingles with the wine at the altar, so that our humble acts of reparation and our sacrifice may become one with the sacrifice of our Saviour, and his oblation and ours be one single oblation."

Our Lord called her to shed not only drops of water, but her life-blood. Father Calage had said: " The foundation of this work will be laid only upon a ground strewn with victims. . . ." Mother Mary of Jesus herself was the first to fall, shot by an anarchist on February 27, 1884.

Another pre-eminently Eucharistic soul was Thérèse Durnerin. She did not belong to the family of Mother Deluil-Martigny, for she was the foundress of the Congregation of the *Amis des Pauvres*, but she expressed herself in very similar terms concerning our union as victims with our Lord.

" To communicate is not the action of a moment; it is a mystery of love towards which the whole of our lives as Christians should gravitate. It is, in reality, an uninterrupted sacrifice . . . our Redeemer having at last found those who will co-operate in his work of redemption, without whom he cannot apply its merits to the world." Her biographer continues: " Jesus has need of this bread purged of the old leaven, and these souls who have abandoned themselves to the divine will he changes into himself. Thus the more a soul dies to itself, by acts of mortification, the more fit is it to become a living host."

No period, perhaps, has seen so many pure-minded and loving souls fashioned after this likeness. It is not only Holy Communion that assists us to a fuller comprehension of our Lord's designs in the Holy Eucharist, and in particular of his desire to unite us to his perpetual work of redemption, but also the devotion to the Sacred Heart. In many ways the two devotions become united to form one. The latter, however, enables us to realise more readily the anguish of the beloved Master at the sight of the appalling uselessness of his redemption.

Allusion has been made already to the grief which our Lord must have felt in the Agony and during his Three Hours on the Cross. The devotion to the Sacred Heart is not a devotion to a picture or statue. It is a devotion to a real Heart, to the love of a man who loves us with the love of a God. It implies love that voluntarily consents not to receive all the return that is its due, so that generous souls may be able to assist in the work of redemption. In meditating upon the Sacred Heart, the Christian gains a more intimate knowledge of his hidden sorrow and of his mercy, and he realises what he is called upon to do in return.

The devotion to the Holy Face, closely akin to devotion to the Sacred Heart, owes much to the energetic propaganda of Monsieur Dupont, the holy man of Tours. By this means many have been led to a truer estimation of the value of the act of St Veronica when she wiped the face of our Lord. Many women, remembering what she did, have desired to imitate her; many men, not willing to be behindhand, have taken Simon the Cyrenean as their model.

Owing to these, and other less apparent influences, people have begun to realise that in the history of the salvation of the human race there are great opportunities for their own individual efforts. A complete theological treatise on the work of Christ the Redeemer, unless it be sadly mutilated, must of necessity include the study of the redemption both in the Person of Christ the *head* and in the *members* of Christ the *head*.

The greater appreciation of the *Liturgy* has been another potent auxiliary. It has widened the outlook, and by emphasising the communal and

social aspect of prayer, helped men to a better
conception of the unity of the Church. The unsus-
pected depths of the union of Christ with his
members has received greater attention. Christians
have begun to see more clearly the significance
of the fact that nearly all the Church's prayers,
beginning with the Our Father, and including the
majority of those contained in the Mass, are written
in the plural number.

But the spirit of self-sacrifice is not found only
in the Holy Eucharist, it may be discovered also
in Holy Baptism, where before receiving the Holy
Eucharist the recipient is already consecrated to a
life of self-immolation.

The study, or at anyrate the influence, of the French
spiritual writers of the seventeenth century favoured
these discoveries Men were enabled to understand
how, to quote the words of Senault in his book
*L'Homme chrétien, ou la Réparation de la nature par
la grâce,* " the Christian religion, by converting man
into a victim, obliges him to make the sacrifice of
his whole being to God. The Christian fails in his
most ordinary duties if he does not lead a life of
self-sacrifice. Since he is composed of soul and
body, he ought to sacrifice both the one and the
other, so as to have the honour of being a perfect
burnt-offering."

It may be added that the more general practice
of meditation and of retreats, by deepening their
knowledge of Christian doctrine, has enabled many
to appreciate our Lord's action in our own spiritual
lives, and his need of our assistance in the work of the
world's salvation. " Anyone in the school of Christ
who concludes his studies before he has reached
the cross will not have finished the course," says
Monsignor Gay. Every time that we examine
closely into the Christian religion we find ourselves
at the hard bedrock of self-renunciation. It remains

but to find the best method of using this solid building material for the construction of vast structures
wherein, thanks to our efforts, multitudes may take
refuge and find the God whom they are seeking.

CHAPTER III

RESULTS

At no period of the Christian era have there been so
many religious congregations and isolated individuals
whose lives are devoted to the apostolate of self-
sacrifice as at the present day.

I

There are two ways of approaching a life of self-
sacrifice. We may either offer to make the best use
of self-sacrifice for the sake of love, or we may
offer ourselves to be used as fully as possible by
divine Love himself.

In the first case we promise out of love to obey the
will of God as made known to us in the commandments, in the obligations of our state, in duties of
charity and the rest, and to correspond always with
the clearly understood will of God.

In the second case we promise, out of love, to
accept all the opportunities for the crucifying of self
that may occur.

Many will be found who are willing to offer themselves for one or other of these forms of self-immolation, with the intention of giving to Christ the supple-
mentary aid he demands in the work of redemption.

The life of Pauline Reynolds is an example, among
many others, of the most generous self-sacrifice for
the good of souls, and especially of those souls in
whom fidelity is most necessary. She entered

Carmel at the age of fifty-seven, having been obliged until that time to remain in the world to help her mother.   At Montmartre our Lord made known to her that he desired her to become a daughter of St Teresa.   At the pilgrimage of La Salette, he told her the reason.   " Thou shalt become a Carmelite for the sake of my priests."

" I understood," she says, " that Jesus made me responsible for the souls of his ministers whom I should be able to aid, to raise out of their lethargy, to save and sanctify by my life as a Carmelite. This mission had been entrusted to me already, but I had not fully understood nor accepted it until that morning.   ' Thou shalt become a Carmelite for the sake of my priests.'   Except what holy obedience may enjoin, all is for them.   These are precious jewels for our Lord; I must set to work and polish them and make them shine. . . .   Every action in my life shall be sealed with these words of our Lord, which I take as my motto, and the inspiration of all my intentions: ' and for them do I sanctify myself, that they may be sanctified in truth.'[1] . . .   I feel, while writing these words, that by them I shall be judged.   Have pity upon me, O Lord, but I do not wish to take anything back.   Whether in life or in death, all I have is for thy priests."

Madeleine de Remusat was born at Marseilles in 1696, six years after the death of St Margaret Mary.   When she was still at school our Lord appeared to her and told her he was looking for a victim.   The child suggested to him one of her mistresses who seemed to her most edifying.   " No, it is not she whom I want," was the reply.   Then she proposed someone else, but the answer was: " Thou art the victim I desire."   She lived the life of a saint in the midst of acute physical sufferings; sometimes she had attacks of coughing that lasted

[1] St John xvii 19.

continually for five hours. She died in the Visitation
Order at the age of thirty-three.

" I am looking for a victim." These were the
words which our Lord addressed to St Margaret
Mary. " I am looking for a victim who is willing to
sacrifice herself for the fulfilment of my designs.
Wilt thou give me thy heart as a refuge for my suffering heart which is despised by all men ?"

And what response will be made by generous
souls ? There are offers of help from all sides, such
as our Lord was hoping to receive when he made his
pitiful and reiterated appeal.

Xavierine de Maistre writes:

" My God and my all, I realise thy mysterious
operations in my soul, I have heard thy appeal, and
behold me, I am ready. I offer myself to thee to be
thy victim in the full acceptance of the term. I
deliver over to thee my body, my soul and my heart,
and all that I have, so that thou mayest sacrifice
them to thy good pleasure. I offer thee my life;
take it, my God. Love lays down no conditions
or reservations, and I make none. My most tender
Father, I offer myself to thee and beseech thee to
accept me. Do not consult either my preferences or
my dislikes; if thy love is content, that will be
sufficient. When I think of my own frailty, I am
frightened; but when I turn to thee, my sweet and
tender Lord, I feel myself strengthened and irresist-
ibly drawn towards a life of complete self-immolation. I distrust myself, but I trust in thee. Mary,
my good and tender mother, have pity upon thy
child. She is alarmed . . . but in spite of her fears,
she wants to bring glory and consolation to her God.
Offer me, I beseech thee, to the most holy and most
adorable Trinity. I desire to have the purity of thy
pure heart so as to be worthier of the God to whom
I make my oblation. Mary, obtain for me the favour
that each day the number of my failings may grow

less. May I attain the degree of perfection marked out for me by the Holy Trinity, so that I may live my life out of pure love. Lastly, may I receive the grace of final perseverance. O angels of heaven, ye saints, and especially my holy patrons and patronesses, tell my beloved King that here is his chosen victim, who delivers herself to his love for ever."

The following prayer, composed by Thérèse de Couderc, the foundress of the *Ladies of the Cenacle*, reveals the guiding principle of her life:

" Lord Jesus, I unite myself to thy perpetual, unceasing and universal sacrifice. I offer myself to thee for my whole life, and every moment of every day to do thy most adorable and holy will. Thou didst become a victim for my salvation; I wish to become a victim of thy love. Accept my desire and my offering, and grant my petition that I may die of love, that the last beating of my heart may be an act of perfect love."

We have already spoken of the Eucharistic character of this attraction to a life of self-sacrifice. Marie Pérignon, an associate of the nuns of Perpetual Adoration at the mother house at Paris, drew up the following rule of life:

" To be a host for our Lord the Eucharistic Host. As he delivered up and gave himself, to deliver and give myself in return. To give myself at every moment as he is given and is exposed to view at every moment of the day. To give myself as bread is given to us, as the flour which is crushed in the mill. To give myself as the host is given to the priest, broken. To give myself, as Christ is given in each particle, whole and entire. To give myself so that from my death these others may be born anew, and by our lives rather than by our words they may be led to the source of living water."

Some objectors may declare that this is convent

phraseology, but similar expressions may be heard in the trenches or from a hospital bed.

Bernard Lavergne, who was killed in the attack of September, 1915, a few days before made the offering of his future life as priest; he wrote saying:

" I am moved when I think of those whom God accepts as substitutes, concerning whom he alone knows the hidden mystery, of those lives prematurely ended, the sacrifice of which has purchased victories of infinite value."

Another brave soldier, who was forced to have both of his legs amputated, wrote:

" The month of the Sacred Heart brings me happiness: it is true that I am always in pain, but to suffer has become almost a necessity for my happiness." An army chaplain, formerly a missionary in Madura, wrote to the sorrow-stricken mother:

" Your tears have their place in my chalice; in very truth they complete the sacrifice of our Saviour. The words of St Paul: ' I fill up those things that are wanting . . . ' are being verified to the letter. I am living amidst sacrifices, bloody holocausts. Let us unite our sacrifices for our Lord and the good of souls."

War against the foreigner does not last for ever. But there are other forms of combat such as the struggle against self which takes place in our drab and uninteresting daily life, and is devoid of all the trappings of heroism. Madame Marie Lucie Vrau, the wife of Camille Féron-Vrau, was a woman living in the world. But from her earliest years God called her to a close union with himself. In 1876, he made known to her the special vocation of making reparation which he had entrusted to her. Her response was to take a vow on March 15, 1878, offering herself as a victim in these words:

" Lord Jesus, Divine Redeemer, prostrate at thy feet, and trusting in thy merciful tenderness, I

consecrate myself to thee to be thy victim.   I accept
in advance, and of my own free will, for love of thee
and in union with thee, all the sufferings and pains,
whether of body or of soul, that it may please thee
to send me.   I accept them fully, in response to thy
designs upon me, and to the urgent invitations of
thy Sacred Heart.   I accept them in the spirit of
reparation, in expiation for my sins, and to make
amends for the outrages committed by sinners
against thy glory.   I accept them in order to obtain
graces for the Sovereign Pontiff and for Holy
Church.   I make this vow for life; and I promise
under pain of sin never to revoke it, and to live
each day according to its spirit."

" MARIE LUCIE VRAU."

She added a complete offering of her whole being,
which closed with these words:

" Jesus-Host, be in me the person, the substance,
the guiding principle of my life, and its final end.
Let me be only the envelope, thy member and
instrument, like the humble and pure species in the
Blessed Sacrament."

On December 16, 1879, she writes:

" Jesus said to me, ' See how I love these souls !   It
is out of love that I thus give myself: I want many
souls.'   Then he made known to me his immense love
for men, and his great desire and burning thirst
that they should draw near and receive him in Holy
Communion.   He showed me the longing of his
Sacred Heart, and at the same time caused me to
understand and experience the grief that he suffered
at the sight of so many people who repulse his tender
advances. . . .   Jesus said to me: ' Give me
souls ' "

Her whole life—she died on December 13, 1913—
was offered to " fill up those things that are wanting
to the Passion of Christ."   She had fully understood

the words which our Lord addressed to another
privileged soul:

" My heart desires to find souls who with me, in
me, and by me, are willing to become great victims
for God, who will aid me to save the world, and to
regenerate and vivify humanity. They shall agree
to live their lives as I live mine in the Host, lives
consecrated to the glory of the Father and the
salvation of souls. . . ."

The bitterest pain which affects the Sacred Heart
is caused by these souls who are his, and are walking
in the way of perfection. . . . Yet are they inspired
by the spirit of self - seeking, so that they forget
that by their vocation and special privileges they
are bound to make expiation and intercession, and
therefore no longer belong to themselves.

Maggie, a young Belgian girl, offered herself as a
victim to God for the protection of her Franciscan
brother in the Great War. Her desire was not so
much to safeguard a precious life, as to further the
welfare of the many souls who would be saved if the
life of the friar was preserved in battle.

Still younger was Marguérite, a member of the
Children's Crusade at Namur. At the age of eleven,
God led her along the royal way of the cross.

" If you ask God to cure me, let it be for the
intention of our dear missions; if not, may Jesus give
me as much pain to bear as possible. Everything
I have to suffer is for foreign missions. I never say
to Mother that I feel ill, only sometimes she guesses.
Then she tries to relieve me; this causes me more
pain, for it is only when I am very ill that I feel that
the good God is spoiling me. When I speak to our
Lord, I call myself always, Marguérite of foreign
missions, or Marguérite of the Cross. I should like
to merit both of these names. Pray that I may be
very good, and above all that I may suffer and work
hard for Jesus and our dear negroes."

It must not be thought that the fact of our clearly defined share in the work of our Lord's redemption is based upon these private revelations, however authentic they may be. It rests upon the dogmatic truth of our incorporation with Christ in his mystical body.

Yet it may be of interest to note how continually, and more especially during the nineteenth century, our Lord is reminding us of this truth.

It is necessary to be extremely suspicious of individual revelations, especially those which lack a dogmatic foundation. Even when the text of the revelation brings to light some doctrinal point, this is not thereby a necessary proof of its divine origin, although it may give a prima facie probability that it is authentic, or at any rate be a guarantee of its harmless character. There are two extremes to be avoided: to accept everything as certain, or to reject everything as disproved. There are many hysterical people in the world, but there are also others who are quite level-headed. The divine action must not be unduly minimised by including everything that claims to be a revelation from God in a general condemnation. At that rate we should have to reject St Gertrude's *Herald of Divine Love*, the *Revelations* of St Mary Magdalen of Pazzi, the *Book of Visions* of Blessed Angela of Foligno, and the *Dialogues*, and what a loss they would be !

If all mystical writings were proscribed, the Church would run the risk of being deprived of many highly valuable data concerning our Lord's dealings with individual souls. The important point is to know how to distinguish the true mystic from the false. This is a delicate task certainly, but of what use to the serious-minded director are his theological and moral training unless among other advantages they enable him to detect the difference? This remark is not intended to justify from a critical point of view all the passages quoted in this volume, but to prevent the wholesale condemnation of mystical writings. No one, however unwilling to accept the confidences of the interior life, will contest the psychological value of the *Journal* of Elizabeth Leseur. She offered her life for the conversion of her husband, and every reader of those pages knows the wonderful manner in which God took her at her word.

The life of Sister Madeleine Ulrich has been published under the title of *Une Victime d'amour au Sacré Cœur de Jésus*. The following passages, if they can be credited, are taken from our Lord's revelations to her:

" The moment has arrived when my glory requires reparation and satisfaction to be made. The time has come when mercy should give place to justice. It is now that justice has to be appeased by the homage of reparation which you must offer. I have chosen you for this purpose, you, my priests, and all you who in your hearts experience the anguish which tore my heart on Calvary, and the thirst for reparation for my Father's glory, out of love for the souls of men who will not understand what is for their happiness on earth and their eternal felicity in heaven."

Our Lord used similar words to Thérèse Durnerin:

" I am just when someone has fulfilled his own personal task. I take the overplus of his expiatory works as my divine right. I unite them to my supernatural merits, and out of the accumulation of my acts of expiation and those of my elect I build up a treasure which I jealously guard. This is the reason for those acts of excessive mortification which make the lives of my predestined a perpetual martyrdom. I hurry on the work and increase their sufferings, judging it to be good from the divine standpoint. Much labour is necessary in order that the divine life may spring forth anew in poor human nature."

The words of the foundress of the *Amis des Pauvres* show that she was inspired by the same interior solicitations.

" O for some souls that are not merely tender-hearted, but also generous-minded, who yearn to prove their love for Jesus by their lives of penance. They are needed to awaken those others who are slumbering in lethargy and in the self-absorbed routine of their own personal well-being. Victims are required. Jesus is seeking them. No more can he bear suffering in his glorified body, so his wounded Heart looks for souls from whom he can obtain the graces needed for raising to life those who are in danger of losing their souls. The decisive hour has arrived. The good have suffered great things, and their acts of expiation and reparation are about to receive their reward. But if definite victory is to be won, there must be martyrs who will make the free-will sacrifice of their lives out of love, for the triumph of Jesus the Host. The scales of justice are waiting for the acts of heroism of the just. At this price only can the terrible evils with which the enemy threatens them be averted. Let us become victims, so that in us Jesus can fill up what is wanting to his Passion, and thus redeem the world which is losing itself in the mire."

There are a number of other examples that suggest themselves: Mother Marie de Jésus, foundress and first prioress of the *Carmelite Convent* at *Paray-le-Monial*; Hélène de Chappotin de Neuville, foundress of the *Franciscan Sisters of Mary*, whose name in religion, Mother Mary of the Passion, clearly denotes her devotion to the Cross; Elizabeth of the Trinity; St Thérèse of the Child Jesus, who offered herself as a victim to his merciful love. She declared: " To receive martyrdom was the dream of my childhood, and has increased now that I am in my little cell at Carmel. But my folly has become greater, for it is not only one form of suffering that I desire, but I can be satisfied only with every kind of torment." Another Carmelite, Sister Mary of Jesus Crucified, a lay nun, performed heroic acts of mortification bordering sometimes on the bizarre. Mother Ponnet, of the *Visitation Convent* at *Vaisseaux*, Sister Mary of St Anselm of the community of the *White Sisters in Africa*—we will not add to the list, lest it be thought to be all-inclusive.

These examples are a mere handful taken at random, but they are sufficient, perhaps, to serve their purpose, and may encourage us to make a closer survey which, although incomplete—for the finest instances will remain hidden—yet will be more comprehensive.

A similar list can be made of persons living in the world: Seraphine Adèle, whose memoirs, entitled *Une âme victime et hostie*, speak for themselves; Michelle Folin, a Christian mother who died at the age of eighty-three after a life of self-sacrifice; Carmen de Sojo, a noble Spanish lady, who performed heroic acts of penance.

In all these cases the motive is not only the love of sacrifice, but the love of sacrifice as redemptive and as complementary of the work of redemption. In some instances it is the love of souls that leads them to imitate the sufferings of Christ. With others it is love of our Lord which impels them to sacrifice themselves for the good of souls, and often, very often, these two motives are combined. The individual thus becomes a benefactor in two ways. He assists our Lord and aids his fellow-man; the piece of money has two sides, but it is one and the same coin. It aids Christ and it redeems humanity.

The following passages, taken from the life of Thérèse Durnerin, are very convincingly and plainly expressed:

" When people offer themselves to our Lord as

victims, they are always taken at their word. It is impossible to foresee the lengths to which this voluntary sacrifice of self will lead them. It is always the most sensitive part which is attacked. Suddenly we find ourselves like victims about to be slaughtered by the executioner. But it is not the executioner that we should see, but the divine High Priest who wields the knife. We have offered ourselves as victims, and he makes full use of us. It is as if Mass were being offered in our individual souls; the heart is the altar whereon our Lord is hourly renewing his mystical sacrifice."

It is not sacrifice as such that saves humanity, but sacrifice in so far as it is a manifest proof of love. The abbess of Solesmes, Mother Cécile, explains this point to her nuns:

" God and his will are the only absolute good; suffering is only a relative good. It will not exist in heaven, and in this world, although it is a method of showing our love, it is by no means indispensable. In itself suffering is not meritorious, and unless it is united to love it is not Christian, but mere stoicism."

II

Hitherto we have dealt with separate individuals; now it is time to pass on to the consideration of the various religious congregations whose special object is a life of reparation.

To come under this category it is not necessary that they should openly bear this title. Bourdaloue says in one of his books that to be a religious and a victim is one and the same thing. Certainly it is quite possible to be a monk or a nun and for the spirit of self-sacrifice to have no part or a very small one in the daily life. This is a failure to live up to vocation which in no way detracts from the truth of the theory. If we consider the religious life and

what it entails without any additions, it will be seen
that it includes sufficient for complete martyrdom,
and therefore for *copiosa redemptio*. In the ordinary
daily round of the Christian life there are many
opportunities of self-renunciation for those who
know how to find and use them.

Fifteen years after the death of Madame Louise
of France, the daughter of Louis XV, there came
to the Carmelite convent of the rue de Grénille in
Paris another great lady who asked permission to
lead a life of reparation for the King of France.

" Do you know anything about our life ?" asked
the Prioress at the first interview. " Do you like
fish ?" " I hate it," she answered vehemently.
" And eggs?" " I detest them ! I keep abstinence
on Fridays, but frequently on Saturdays I have a
headache." " Then how can you possibly become
a Carmelite ?" " I shall do penance, and that is all
I want." And this postulant with her delicate
digestion passed more than fifty years in the Carmelite convent, without mitigating any of the austerities
included in their rule. Nearer our own times there
came another would-be postulant to ask to be received, and to her also were put the same questions.
She asked: " Is there a crucifix in the cell ?"
" Yes." " Then do not question me further; all
that is required of me I shall do." In the Carmelite
cell there is only a plain cross; the figure of Christ
is absent to show each inhabitant that it is she
herself who has to be nailed to the wood of the
cross.

When Anne Eugènie Milleret de Brou, the daughter
of an official receiver, came to Lacordaire to consult
him about her vocation, he said: " Do you know
the Congregation of the Order of Mercy ? It consists of men who, knowing there are human beings
living in slavery, offer themselves and sacrifice their
liberty in order to free them. This is the meaning

9

(discarded)

of the religious life; it is the giving of self for the salvation of souls." And he added: " Pray and wait." The result of this delay and these prayers was the foundation of the *Congregation of the Augustinians of the Assumption.*

The various religious congregations that were founded during the nineteenth century were all inspired by a motive similar to that expressed by Lacordaire. In every instance the founder or foundress emphasised the importance of becoming a redeemer with Christ. On February 12, 1838, Julie-Adèle of Gérin-Ricard, the first Superior of the *Sœurs Victimes du Sacré-Cœur* at Marseilles, received the following message from her director, the Abbé Beausier:

" God is no longer known, loved or served, souls are falling into hell, the Sacred Heart is torn, his love is scorned. He asks for reparation to be made for all these wrongs. Hence we intend to console the Sacred Heart by offering virgins to him as victims." The discipline of the new Order was to be very strict; the rule was formed by choosing the most perfect elements in the rules of other communities.

The young girl grouped round her three of her friends: at the close of their first formal meeting they made this act of consecration: " We consecrate ourselves entirely to God, and devote ourselves without reserve to accomplishing all that he desires of us in his mercy as also in his justice. . . . And we promise to become victims for our own sins and for those of France in union with Jesus Christ upon the Cross. We consent to suffer with him all the pains he may see fit to send us, and desire even to be chosen as holocausts in expiation for the crimes of our country if it pleases God to accept us. We pledge ourselves to bear suffering and to die in union with our Lord who suffered and died for us."

Two months later the Abbé Beausier sent them a

calendar for the week, in which each day was marked out with a special intention for their work of reparation.

Sunday: Reparation for scandals committed in churches, and for the profanation of Sunday.

Monday: For the violation of the commandments of God and the Church.

Tuesday: For the scorn and misuse of God's word and for resistance to grace.

Wednesday: For human frailty among priests and religious orders.

Thursday: For unworthy Communions.

Friday: For lack of fidelity in keeping the baptismal vows.

Saturday: For sacrilegious confessions.

Later on another priest, the Abbé Arbaumont, who also was attracted towards a life of reparation and expiation, asked to become their chaplain.

We read in the life of Emilie d'Outremont, Countess of Hoogworst, who later became the foundress of the *Congregation of Marie Réparatrice*, that at Strasbourg on July 1, 1857, during Benediction, our Lord asked her for " love and suffering." And in order to respond to this twofold and unique desire of our Lord, she gathered round her other souls, who offered their lives out of love even to the length of sacrifice, a loving sacrifice after the example and with the assistance of Mary the mother of sorrows and queen of martyrs.

Two worthy daughters of such a mother, both of them invalids, realised that their sufferings served to complete the passion of our Saviour, and far from trying to avoid them, generously offered them to God. One of them writes:

" My beloved Master, give me souls that I may be able to give them back to thee, that I may place them in thine arms and say: ' I desire more opportunities for self-immolation if it is necessary for their salvation.' I thank thee, good Master, for the feeling of weariness which comes to us every evening exactly at the hour when people in the world are beginning to amuse themselves."

Sophie de Claye, who lived in more recent times, writes:

" Lord Jesus, thou who knowest both my weakness and my desire to balance the scales of divine justice so that the merited chastisement may be tempered with mercy and love. Vouchsafe to open thine ears to the promises which under thine inspiration I offer thee with all my heart. In order that sinners may pray, in order that official France may pray, I no longer ask for consolations in my prayers. I desire to be deprived of the divine light and to accept darkness and spiritual aridity, so that France, the eldest daughter of the Church, may become Christian once more."

Here is the most painful form of self-immolation. To ask to be deprived of creatures is comprehensible, it is nothing. But to give up the realisation of God's presence means the sacrifice of all that is worth having.

The Franciscan Missionaries of Mary, when they make their profession, add the following words: " I offer myself as a victim for the Church and for the good of souls."

Mother Thérèse of the Cross, foundress of the *Gardiennes Adoratrices* of St Aignan, understood that for the foundation of her special work she had to become " a victim for the honour and glory of the Holy Eucharist." On Maundy Thursday, 1862, she promised to ask God for sufferings and humiliations, and never to refuse any sacrifice, but rather to choose out of two courses open to her the one which would cost her the more. The divine Master inspired her with so keen an appreciation of the value of self-sacrifice for the good of souls that she asked all her daughters to offer themselves as victims for this object.

These individuals and religious communities who offer themselves for the apostolate of self-sacrifice know perfectly well that they are not doing something which is outside the ordinary interpretation of the Catholic spirit, or a work of supererogation. They know that this is merely a part of the normal machinery, so to speak, of the Church. Those who are appointed to the apostolate of the spoken word need the support of a reserve store of acts of self-renunciation and of prayer. The vocation to a life of self-sacrifice is a work of the first importance in the economy of the Church; it is the source of great riches, and supplies many complex needs.

The foundress of the work of Adoration and Reparation, Mother Marie Thérèse, said:

" I consider this work to be rather the perfect expression of the Christian spirit than a new development."

No one is a perfect Christian unless he can say, in the words of St Paul: " I fill up those things that are wanting . . .," and unless he resolutely devotes himself to this form of apostolate according to the divine Will and in proportion to his own capacity.

It is because so many persons neglect their vocation as co-redeemers that our Lord asks of others, who realise their obligations, a greater measure of generosity and unquestioning self-devotion.

The Helpers of the Holy Souls include in their prayers and acts of self-renunciation not only the Church militant, but also the suffering Church; no part of the Communion of Saints is omitted. " Pray, love, and suffer " is the motto of the Order, which the foundress was the first to put into practice in a most exemplary manner.

For a long time she met with many external difficulties; then interior suffering came to her.

" Good Jesus, I bow down under a cross whose name I know not. Grant that I may allow myself to be crucified. I feel the pains of thy Passion in my soul. Give me a love of self-sacrifice and of suffering. Take me, stretch me out upon thy cross, I am thy victim; but give me courage, Jesus, to bear thy loving chastisement."

When her congregation was established physical suffering again attacked her, and seemed as if it would paralyse her power of action. She turned for advice to the Curé d'Ars; the Abbé Tocanier, his curate, sent her his reply:

" The Curé is astonished that after offering yourself as a victim for the souls in purgatory you should doubt that it is the divine Will for you to suffer. ' Tell her,' he says, ' that the good God desires her to suffer this martyrdom in order to bring down his blessing upon her and her household.' "

Sufficient examples have been given to show that in each century the Cross has been beloved. At the present day the love of Christ crucified is certainly not less profound, although, perhaps, it is accompanied by a deeper theological understanding than at other periods.

Some regret the use or rather the misuse of the term "victim." And in point of fact it is a word that has been misused. But when a certain term or its exaggeration is condemned, we must be careful not to reject the underlying truth, which in this case is nothing more nor less than the practice of Christianity led to its logical conclusion. As St John Eudes has said: " Baptismal grace is the grace of martyrdom."

There are many moral evils at the present day, but are they any worse than in preceding generations? At any rate, the generosity of chosen souls is in no way diminished. There is certainly at the present time a more general tendency among good Christians to seek after a deeper appreciation of the motives that dictate a life of generous self-renunciation.

God be praised if this modest little volume may be of assistance in furthering this good result.

EPILOGUE

MONTALEMBERT, moved by the memory of his parting with his daughter when she left him to take up a life of self-sacrifice, gave to the world the following epic expression of his grief:

"Who is this invisible Lover, who died upon the Cross eighteen hundred years ago, who can thus draw to himself youth, beauty, and love; who reveals himself with so strong an attraction that he is irresistible; who captures her and makes her his slave? Is it a man? No, it is God; a God alone can triumph thus. This is Jesus whose divinity is every day insulted or denied, who is proved to be God by this miracle of disinterested love and courage and by many other signs. Young and innocent persons give themselves to him in return for the gift that he has made of himself. This sacrifice which causes us so much pain is but the response of finite love to the love of a God who was crucified for love of us."[1]

These celebrated words, written fifty years ago, find their echo in less well-known words from the pen of the great Napoleon. The Emperor was stupefied by the thought that it was by the cross our Lord had chosen to spread abroad his kingdom; for him it was a proof of his divinity.

"Christ expected success through his death on the cross. Could this be man's invention? . . . He said: 'They will take me and crucify me: I shall be forsaken by all men, my death will be life unto my disciples; the spirit of the Cross will help them to understand my Gospel and to publish it abroad.

[1] *The Monks of the West*, by Montalembert, vol. v.

They will believe in it and preach it, and will persuade the whole world of its truth.' This absurd promise, which St Paul has rightly named the folly of the Cross, this prophecy made by a wretched crucified malefactor, has been literally fulfilled. And the manner of its fulfilment is, perhaps, an even greater wonder than the promise itself. It was neither the work of a single day, nor a decisive battle that decided the issue. I do not see any army, but some mysterious energising power, and a few men scattered here and there in all quarters of the globe, with no other rallying point except a common faith in the mystery of the Cross. What a strange symbol! The very instrument of torture of the God-man. It is with this that his disciples are armed. They carry the cross throughout the world as a sign of their faith, like a burning flame that spreads from one place to another. Can you imagine a dead person being able to make such conquests; who has soldiers without pay, without hope of reward in this world, who yet is able to inspire them with the desire to persevere and suffer all kinds of privations?"

Our Saviour must needs be all-powerful to be able to draw souls to the extreme limit of self-renunciation: no less than the omnipotence of God is required.

This is the first lesson to be learned from this book, which, although it may be over-prolific in its quotations, yet succeeds in expressing its theme.

*   *   *   *   *

There is a second lesson to be taken to heart.

Such lengths of folly are not for us, we say. We can admire them; imitate them we cannot. There are many different ways in which we may imitate them. Great opportunities, perhaps, are not for us. And it is better that this should be so, for perhaps we should not know how to act if they came. But there remain many smaller occasions which can be used by any generous-minded soul.

No reader of these pages will be content to lead a life of mediocrity. He will wish to give our Lord a large measure of his love. Therefore he must not try to avoid every cross. " A life without the cross is a loveless life." Let him take courage from the example of his Master, and remember the words: " If any man will come after me, let him deny himself and take up his cross and follow me "[1]—the cross of faithful observance of the commandments, the cross of his daily duties, and especially the cross of keeping steadfastly in a state of grace. There is much implied by this last injunction, for, as has been said, " the state of grace is an heroic state."

At times the bearing of our daily cross and all that it involves, even when narrowed down within the strictest limits, will seem to be a heavy burden.

We should often remind ourselves of these great devotees of a life of self-sacrifice, those mentioned in this volume, and thousands of others whose lives can be studied at leisure.

Our eyes should gaze frequently upon the great cross of our Master, which in its divine majesty dominates the cross of his saints. St Teresa said that meditation upon the Passion was one of the surest guarantees of predestination.

Anyone who visits the chapel of Newman at Birmingham will be struck by the enormous crucifix which looks as if it would fall down and crush the altar. Newman had a great deal to suffer, and he wished to have before him, when he prayed, a large crucifix out of all proportion, indeed, to the size of the chapel, but in proportion to the dimensions of his own troubles.

A similar motive inspired the defenders of the section of Bois-le-Prêtre in the Great War. When

[1] St Matt. xvi 24.

they had to alter the line of trenches, they took a crucifix formerly belonging to a Carmelite convent which had been with them in the trench they were abandoning, and placed it in the fresh line, as an incentive to encourage them to hold fast.